UN
AN UNFILTERED GUIDE TO
BX
CREATING A CAREER ON YOUR TERMS
ED

UN

AN UNFILTERED GUIDE TO

BX

CREATING A CAREER ON YOUR TERMS

ED

NICK MURPHY

PST Media Group

ISBN: 978-1-7335867-0-2

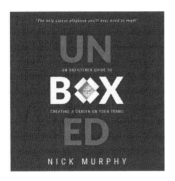

Download the Audiobook Free!

READ THIS FIRST

Just to say thanks for buying my book, I would like to give you the Audiobook version 100% FREE!

TO DOWNLOAD, GO TO:

www.nickmurphy.io/unboxed

IT'S YOUR TURN TO GET UNBOXED

Before you start reading:

Download the Unboxed companion workbook for free at **www.nickmurphy.io/unboxed-readers** to gain access to additional tips, resources, and worksheets that you'll need to create a career on your terms.

DEDICATION

To my kids,

May you always follow your heart,
curiosity, and passion towards creating fulfilling lives
that give you purpose while providing you
security and unending happiness each and
every day. You are the loves of my life
and I know you will each thrive in your own
unique way.

Love always,
—Daddy

CONTENTS

FOREWORD

You're about to experience an amazing story. In fact, if you're willing to, you're about to re-author your own story of how you most profoundly want the role of career to play in your life.

As an Executive Coach, I challenge high performers to define success on a daily basis. I don't think I could possibly love Nick's definition of success any more: living your life on your own terms.

I chose my vocation because I am of the firm belief that none of us needs to settle for life on less than our terms. I believe we are designed to thrive, not just survive. And yet, according to research on American job satisfaction, it has remained consistently true for decades that the vast majority of us aren't thriving at all.

TGIF and all that nonsense. And then Monday morning rolls around and it's time to get back to "the grind." Too many of us are settling, struggling, and often worse, suffering in careers that don't fulfill us. That's not only tragic, but wholly unnecessary.

Before reading *Unboxed* I assumed the title was playing off the cliché of thinking outside the corporate box. After reading my advanced copy, however, I hear the term "unboxed" in a much more powerful way. It's not about thinking "outside" the box, but rather destroying the illusion that the box ever existed in the first place.

Once you become *Unboxed*, you can create success for yourself, on your terms, without being beholden to any corporation, boss, or toxic ideal about what success *should* be. That's pure freedom. And in the rapidly changing "New World of Work," that awareness—that ability—is mission critical.

Fasten your seat belt though, because Part I of this book is going to scare you straight! Nick unapologetically lays out raw data on the impact external forces are having on the workplace. He has clearly done his research, and quite honestly, the future sounds pretty darn bleak. And it will be bleak if you operate from the mindset that you're stuck and there's nothing you can do other than keep looking for better jobs and hope that technology doesn't render you obsolete.

Nick isn't a pessimist bearing bad news. But he's not an optimist either. The message of *Unboxed* is even more powerful than that—it's one of creation.

As William Arthur Ward once said:

> *The pessimist complains about the wind.*
> *The optimist is sure it will go away.*
> *But the creator sets his sails and flies across the sea.*[1]

To the pessimist, the wind (or any obstacle) is just a complete pain in the ass. The optimist is eternally hopeful that all negativity will ultimately pass. But the most successful of them all, the creator, knows that, armed with the proper skills and the right mindset, you can create excellence from within any set of circumstances.

Unboxed is not a book you simply read. This is a book

you DO. In Part II, Nick presents a step-by-step guide on how to reinvent yourself, which is accompanied by a value-packed workbook that walks you through every detail of the three-step plan. Be sure to DO the exercises. It is from that work that the real transformation and liberation will occur.

I truly believe that you can make great money, in a meaningful and rewarding way, and have your life on your terms doing anything as long as it solves a problem and provides a useful service—even if that involves designing and marketing a vest for chickens to wear so they don't die from a sex injury. (I'm not making that up. It's in the book.)

The professional landscape is rapidly and dramatically changing. That is either a serious problem or an unbelievable opportunity, depending on your mindset.

I'm confident that if you take the lessons laid out in *Unboxed* to heart and work to apply them to your life, you are guaranteed to find more fulfillment and success in your career. By the end of your journey, you will have created a life on your own terms, and you'll enjoy the flexibility, freedom, confidence, and pride that come along with that life-changing achievement.

Now it's time to get started.

Create Miracles!

—Chris Dorris
Author of *Creating Your Dream*
and *The Daily Dose: Mental Toughness Tips
in 30 Seconds or Less*

INTRODUCTION

Whether you've been in your career for a few months or a few decades, chances are you've pondered your future more than a handful of times.

Is this job going to get me where I want to go?

How will I develop new skills and get promoted if I'm spending all my time in this one role?

What would I do if my job was eliminated?

I wish I had more freedom and flexibility in my career.

I'd like to be my own boss someday, but I don't see how that's even possible.

I wish I could make money doing what I love . . .

By picking up this book you have the opportunity to create a life and career on your terms, working on the things and with the people you care most about. But to change your career trajectory, you need to break away from the status quo and start to think and work differently than you have up to this point. Problem is, no one has ever shown you how.

To make matters worse, in recent years external forces beyond our control have begun to change the foundation of the way we work as well as the way companies hire. These shifts, some subtle and some obvious, have led many to feel even more uneasy, frustrated, uncertain, and stuck.

I believe everyone deserves a career that provides freedom, flexibility, independence.

I understand how it feels to give your time and energy to a career that takes you away from your family and leaves you with so little freedom and flexibility that it's hard to enjoy the down time you do have because you're so mentally and physically exhausted at the end of each week.

Like you, I once searched high and low for a "better job" and spent years of my prime chasing my tail. Unable to overcome the constant angst I felt, I eventually gave up and walked away from a "stable" corporate job where I made nearly $200k, with five kids to feed, and learned the hard way how to create a career on my terms.

But, if I were starting today, I'd do it differently—and that's what this book is all about. In *Unboxed*, I share what I've learned over more than a decade of doing it the hard way through trial and error so that you can build a career on your terms better and faster than I did.

I've taken my personal experiences from working with thousands of job seekers and dozens of Fortune 500 employers over the last fifteen years and combined them with lessons from business mentors, career experts, and thought leaders in areas from the future of work to mindset, sociology to economics, to create a proven three-step plan that shows you how to create a career on your terms.

This plan has helped thousands of professionals move away from frustration and a lack of control and into certainty, flexibility, and confidence in their career's potential, sustainability, and purpose.

If you're ready to take the first step to shattering your status quo and building a career on your terms, download the free workbook that accompanies *Unboxed* at **www.nickmurphy.io/unboxed-readers** and get ready to change your life.

It's time to stop feeling stuck and unclear about your career and take back control over your life and destiny. It's time to become *Unboxed*.

PART I
THE CASE FOR MAKING CHANGE

"If you have to trade
time for money,
you'll never be wealthy."
—Unknown

CHAPTER ONE:
SETTING THE STAGE

When I was a kid in the 1980s, my dad would put on a suit and tie, give us a sip of his instant breakfast, then kiss my brother and me on the forehead before heading off to his sales job in telecommunications. On most days, he'd leave before we were ready for school and arrive home hours after we did. He also traveled—a lot. He was on a plane three to four times a week.

But he was successful. He won Presidents Club honors in sales, an award given to top sales leaders. He was making $100k back then, roughly equivalent to $200k in today's money. He was promoted time and time again, but, in many ways, he was a slave to his job. His success came at a cost.

In fact, his career would ultimately cost him his marriage.

As I've grown older and become a parent myself, my dad has shared some of his regrets with me: He missed out on baseball practices. He didn't know our morning and evening routines. He seldom, if ever, was home in time to help us with homework. In other words, he didn't have a chance to do all the fatherly things that I now hold dear as a parent.

But this isn't a sob story.

When I was in high school in the late 1990s, my dad, newly remarried, realized that he was tired of trading time for money, so he reinvented his professional self and started an insurance agency. After working his tail off for almost three years, I saw him earn more money than he'd ever earned before. At the same time, I witnessed him having more free time than he'd ever had working in the corporate world. I noticed he was happier, too.

It wasn't until my college years that I began to understand

how deeply his dual work experiences—between corporate and small business ownership—affected my outlook on what I wanted to do with my life. While studying and playing football at Arizona State University, I wasted $2,000 at some sham of a multilevel marketing presentation. After spending all the money I had in the world on products I was never able to sell, I did leave that presentation with one piece of invaluable advice:

"If you have to trade time for money,
you'll never be wealthy."

As soon as I heard that, I instantly thought of my father. He'd somehow escaped the time-for-money trap.

I wondered if I'd ever be able to once college was over. I wanted what he had.

My First Career Transition

After graduation, I became a professional athlete as a punter in the NFL and NFL Europe. During those years, I worried little about my future career aspirations. I was fully fixated on living the dream I had worked so hard to achieve. Everything was about extending my playing career as long as I could.

Unfortunately, as all athletic careers eventually do, that career ended and I found myself out of the NFL by age twenty-six. Along the way, some sort of amnesia set in and I seemed to have forgotten my $2,000 lesson in multilevel marketing. Because what did I do when my playing career ended?

I looked for a job.

But I couldn't find one. When I did get in front of people, I was relatively successful in convincing them that I wasn't a complete moron, but my resumé didn't have the traditional boxes checked. I hadn't had an internship in college. I'd spent four years after graduation kicking an inflated piece of leather—which, as it turns out, is not a highly transferable skill.

While striving in vain even to get interviews, I thought, *I can't be the only person out there struggling with this. What if I made a thirty- to sixty-second video—an elevator pitch—and included it in a job application to supplement my text resumé and really help me tell my unique story? Not so much "Give me the job," but, "Hey, here's some context to my resumé, here's why I deserve an invite to the interview process. This is why I'm worth a conversation."*

So, as someone who'd watched his dad build an insurance business and his mom start a successful yoga studio—and who has always been an innately curious person—I had a lightbulb moment and decided to take action: a friend and I launched WorkBlast, a video resumé company.

During that experience, I learned a ton about the world of work, the broken job-seeker experience, and the ins and outs of talent acquisition and HR. I also saw how companies across all industries look at attracting, engaging, and developing the talent they pay to move their corporate mission forward.

After WorkBlast came to an end, I took what I learned and leveraged that experience to begin a successful corporate career at CareerBuilder, then Monster, then Indeed.com, before going back to entrepreneurship to start my own job site.

Consequently, I've spent more than a decade observing, learning, and working in and around companies with a singular purpose: to get people jobs. These views have been featured on *Inc.*, *USA Today*, the *Wall Street Journal*, Fox Business Network, and HR.com, to name a few. I've been fortunate to become a go-to expert about the world of work.

Which brings us to *Unboxed*. In order to find success in what I've termed the "new world of work," I believe that most people need to unpack almost everything we've been taught about what success looks like in our careers. For generations we've been conditioned to believe that by going to school, earning a degree, and finding a good job, somehow success, or at least stability, is all but guaranteed because our happiness is tied to corporate success. I fundamentally disagree with this as a principle, and the external changes taking place around us are proving that the status quo is untenable.

I don't accept the notion that people, or companies, are best served by putting human being into boxes—whether literally, on an org chart, or figuratively, in terms of pre-defining our contribution to our company and world by looking at our careers in such a narrow scope. In order to survive, let alone thrive by creating success on our terms, we have to be willing to take charge of our career and carve our own path, because for many, the current path is a bridge to nowhere. When you take control of your career and begin to make decisions and plans about what you do for a living, how you do it, and start to operate on your terms, you're becoming *Unboxed*.

The Next Chapter in Employment

Within the last few years, I've seen long-forecasted changes starting to affect people's careers, and I have premonitions about the massive changes looming just a decade or two away—maybe less.

Today, I see a dynamic, complex world with a lot of risks to traditional full-time, 9-to-5 employment.

- Take artificial intelligence and machine learning, for example. Will robots really replace our jobs? What skills will we need to have to compete with AI?

- What about student debt and higher education? Student loan debt is an epidemic, and the cost-benefit analysis of attending college is becoming hard to justify for a lot of people. What does it mean for us—and, more importantly, what can we do about it?
- What about job displacement—whether in coal, manufacturing, retail, or another sector? These jobs are being moved or replaced at an alarming rate.
- And don't forget the impact of offshoring and globalization, or stagnating wage growth, where inflation continues to outpace wage gains at the very same time when being alive is as expensive as ever.

Now, I realize there are plenty of books, articles, and podcasts about these individual topics. But *Unboxed* takes all of those worrisome topics and strives to answer the question you're asking yourself: *what does it mean for me and what can I do about it?*

- How many of these issues are going to significantly disrupt the world of work?

- What happens if two of these issues scale and collide with each other? What will I do for a job then?
- If my job goes away, am I going to have to pay to be re-skilled? How will I know what I want to do? What happens if I just continue to be stuck?
- How do I take control of my own career destiny?

The likely best-case scenario is things continue as they are. But what happens if the status quo is flipped upside down and masses of people are suddenly thrust into underemployment because their full-time job now only requires part-time hours, or worse, unemployment by the pace of change in the new world of work? Can you imagine having a student loan balance on an education that has been deemed irrelevant? How would you pay your bills? Would you have the money to be re-skilled? How long would that take? What new career would you be best positioned for? What if you didn't like it? Could you get assistance in paying for this new education?

Part I seeks to explain why so many of us are unhappy in

our careers, highlight the subtle but significant ways that corporations have changed over the past few decades, and consider the multitude of external forces currently at play that could thwart your future career. I'll also predict what are likely to be the great workforce disruptors of the near future and why you should act today to diversify your career to defend against those forces.

But I won't leave you without hope. While the current environment is littered with looming threats to many jobs of today, technology and globalization provides us with so many more professional possibilities than ever before. In Part II I'll lay out my three-step plan to create a career that works for you on your terms.

Throughout the book, I'll share with you why *now* is the best time—and maybe the only time—you'll have in your career to begin taking steps to guarantee your success and put control of your future firmly back in your own hands. Despite some of the doomsday scenarios I'll present, if you follow my three-step plan you have a great opportunity to serve others, create wealth, make an impact, be fulfilled, and to live life on your own terms. And that's how I define success: living life on your own terms. To me, that means enjoying my work and having a passion for how I spend my time.

Tackling Uncertainty Together

My story, perhaps like yours, still has many chapters yet to be written. But while we wait, I'll share the strategies I've used over the past several years to move away from a six-figure corporate career (with a wife who owns a small business and five kids to feed) and successfully build a career on my terms—a career that gives me full control over how I spend my time and earns me enough money to enjoy life in the places and with the people I love most in this world.

When I consider the realities and inevitabilities that come along with this new world of work, I often wonder what my kids are going to do twenty years from now to earn a decent income. I hope they will be working on something they enjoy, something in which they find fulfillment and purpose. It was pondering this question and reflecting on my journey thus far that led me to write this book in hopes that I can help serve you as you carve your own path, and one day do the same for my kids.

My goal with *Unboxed* is to clarify the impact of what's happening around you and motivate and inspire you to reverse engineer a life and career that allows you the time, flexibility, and income to live the way you want to while not feeling beholden to "the man," or left scrambling for what's next should you find your good, stable job suddenly eliminated. I'll share expert data that will inspire you to act, I'll challenge your conditioned beliefs about what's possible in your career, and I'll encourage and guide you in how to build a career on your terms.

If you're frustrated by where you are, or fear where you might wind up and feel that somewhere along the way you've lost control of your future, today is the day you can take back the power to live and work on your terms.

My sincere hope for everyone who reads this, and for my own children, is that somehow my experience, perspective, and advice can act as the catalyst that leads you to find the answers in your own journey the same way I found mine in my dad's.

"The trouble with being in the rat race is that even if you win, you're still a rat."

−Lily Tomlin

CHAPTER TWO:
WHY YOU'RE UNFULFILLED
AT WORK

According to Gallup, 85 percent of people are unengaged, or actively disengaged in their jobs.[2] This staggering number isn't new information, either. This annual poll has fluctuated between 72–86 percent over the past 30 years!

To make sense of why so many of us feel this way about our careers, it's important to understand that our entire economic system and the lingering effects it has on the way we do our jobs is byproduct of the Industrial Revolution.

The Origin of "The Box"

In the 1776 book *The Wealth of Nations*, Adam Smith argued that the division of labor and employee specialization was the recipe to produce prosperity.[3] Smith famously used the example of making a pin, claiming that by having multiple people focus on one aspect of production, rather than the entire process, productivity and profits would soar.

Prior to this time, most people made their living through craft. There were farmers, traders, blacksmiths, doctors, and the like. Your vocation was closely connected to your way of life, and your trade was your identity because your reputation and standing depended largely on how well you produced and the value you added in the community.

Smith's ideas gained massive popularity, not only because they made sense but also because they were well-timed. New machine technology was being created, and industrialists, no longer bound by waterways and natural power sources, began building factories in cities where thousands of people were conveniently available to supply the labor to run these machines. This was the birth of industrial capitalism.

Unlike Adam Smith, Karl Marx viewed capitalism as

an economic system rooted in commodities. Importantly, he viewed employees as a type of commodity, and since employees have little power or control over the economic system because they don't own the factories, products, and materials themselves, their worth can easily be devalued over time. Marx argued that, by its very nature, capitalism created an imbalance between companies and workers.[4]

According to Marx, the relationship between an employer and their employee is based primarily on conflict, not balance or harmony, even if conflict is a rarer occurrence in the relationship. The company wants maximum output, whereas the employee wants maximum earnings and quality time away from work.

Marx also disagreed fundamentally with Smith and believed that an individual who completed the whole task, compared to only a fraction of it, would care a lot more about the finished product—and presumably the company, the mission, and the outcome of its efforts—than the individual who worked on a single part.

Adam Smith literally created the idea of putting

workers into a box to do a singular task. Because of this, he is widely regarded as the Father of Economics for creating modern-day capitalism. Marx, on the other hand, helps give insight into the natural incongruence between capitalism and the employees companies retain to do the work.

Considering these two diverse economic perspectives has led me to ponder whether people are really meant to function in Smith's world of singular function and specific task. If we were once fulfilled and prosperous as individuals who were defined by the body of our work, it seems incongruent with humanity to strip our work down into too narrow a focus.

Could this be why so many people don't like their jobs? Are we simply not wired to function in this capacity?

The Shift in Corporate Priorities

Once upon a time, we were told that if we went to college, earned a degree, and found a good job at a stable company that we'd be rewarded, protected, even taken care of by our employer. This worked well for people like my late grandfather who worked inside the same insurance company for 41 years until his retirement at age 65. From the end of WWII up to the 1980s, corporations provided stable, long-term employment, health and retirement benefits, and opportunities for upper mobility for the masses. Times were good. In fact, for most of the 20th century, the balance in power of corporations favored both management *and* labor, while shareholders were treated simply as junior partners. It wasn't until the mid-1980s that we began to see a fundamental shift in power away from employees and towards shareholders.

Today, very few firms employ workers who feel as though they're members of an organizational relationship of mutual respect and shared mission with committed long-term owners. Modern corporations have replaced the partnership between management and labor with powerful return-centric shareholders who encourage companies to operate at the lowest possible costs, employing "contractors" who must pay for benefits themselves and who can be hired and fired at will.

Markets have come to celebrate companies that build

shareholder returns on the backs of rented people (employees). In today's world of work, middle-class employees, like my grandfather was, are at risk as much as their working-class peers. Sickness, paternity, and maternity benefits are all pitched at a regulatory minimum, and those companies that do offer anything above the absolute minimum are described as "forward-thinking"—although it clearly seems regressive in the context of work's evolution.

Today, most corporations are, or certainly appear to be, operating from a shareholder-first point of view. These firms have shifted their purpose from building long-term growth through employee partnership to maximizing short-term profit with contractualized workforces. If you feel marginalized by your employer, can you ever be truly fulfilled in your job?

Predictable Dissatisfaction

As much as we may want to condemn organizations for treating their employees like commodities, is it really their fault given the economic systems we've created? Is it possible that capitalism in the 21st century has devolved to a point where, in the absence of stability and mutual respect, employees are no longer willing to tolerate the angst they feel in careers that don't seem to align with their humanity?

If you believe Karl Marx, you may be inclined to argue that people were never designed to work within the confines of an org chart or assembly line in the first place. While working inside these confines may not have felt optimal to people like my grandfather, the incongruence was easier to justify when companies provided stability, security and respect.

Could the erosion of this mutual respect be why 85 percent of employees now report feeling unengaged?

If so, what happens if the jobs we rely on, but no longer love, are threatened?

An Uncertain Future

Close your eyes and fast-forward to the year 2030.

Imagine that 50 percent of all jobs are one-third automatable. Imagine student loan debt outpacing median income. And imagine the jobs of 2030 requiring a higher degree of education than the jobs of today.

Now ask yourself: Will my current job still be around? Will my company? My industry? Will I be able to pay my bills? If I lose my job can I start over? Do I have control over what happens, or is my company in full control of my professional destiny? Should I start thinking about what's next? Do I need additional skills or education? A degree?

The most scientifically based predictions, the most reputable economists and organizations studying the future of work, and some of the smartest minds of our time all agree: big changes are coming.

And when they do, our status quo is going to be flipped upside down.

Don't believe me?

Think back to the Great Recession. Unemployment peaked at 10 percent in October of 2009.[5] As that occurred, jobs went away (some never came back), companies went under and, as a result, people couldn't pay their mortgages. Real estate fell apart, and banks and auto makers needed to be bailed out by the federal government. Markets nearly collapsed. There was utter chaos.

According to the Federal Reserve, the Great Recession only lasted from December of 2007 through June of 2009,[6] but recovery took far longer. Some jobs never recovered. For those of you who lived through it or were young in your careers during the Great Recession, it got really bad. It was scary. Times were uncertain. And a lot of people, especially young people, lost significant income that they will never make up.

The Great Recession was caused primarily by dishonest lending practices which led to a real estate bubble that eventually popped, resulting in a severely debilitating effect on the economy and, consequently, the job market.

If something so damaging to global markets stemmed from one calculated and dishonest "misstep" among bankers, what would happen if multiple external factors intersected at once, creating permanent unemployment, or underemployment, in numbers that dwarf those of the Great Recession?

That's where you could find yourself by 2030.

"You better start swimming
or you'll sink like a stone
for the times
they are a-changing."
—Bob Dylan

CHAPTER THREE:
A PERFECT STORM

Since the 12th century, when feudal lords were forced to create the first paid jobs after the Black Plague wiped out more than 100 million peasants, work has evolved, technology has been created and economic systems have changed. So what is it about today's economic climate that makes this moment in time so unique and potentially dangerous for people who rely solely on a corporate job for their livelihood?

One of my guilty pleasures is a show called *Air Disasters* that airs on the Smithsonian Channel. As someone who loves to travel and flies constantly, it may be odd that I choose to watch so much about planes crashing, but as I've learned, what causes a plane crash is almost never a single failure. It's always a series of failures that happen at exactly the wrong time, compiling issue upon issue, until the airplane is unrecoverable and disaster strikes.

In this chapter, I'll lay out the various external forces at play that create the greatest risk to employees and alert you to the various potential failures that, when combined, create a high likelihood of catastrophe. The good news: unlike an air disaster, we have lots of data and more than mere seconds to make corrections and recover.

Student Loan Debt

Back when I raised $500,000 from friends and family and founded my first start-up, I didn't think I knew anything about finance or accounting at all. So, I decided, in my infinite wisdom, to pursue a Master of Business Administration degree. I didn't have a corporate job that was going to help pay for it, and I wasn't going to be able to pay for it in cash. So, I did what most people do: I took out student loans, thinking to myself,

I'm investing in my education. That's the good kind of debt.

I was accepted into the graduate school program at Arizona State University's WP Carey School of Business. I borrowed a total of $42,000 to pay for my program, including a few thousand dollars in living expenses. While I will never say that I regret having my MBA, what I do regret is the way it was financed. Despite being conditioned to believe student debt was "good debt," I can promise you from experience that there is no such thing as good personal debt.

At its peak in 2016, that same $42,000 loan that was federally subsidized and borrowed through traditional channels, not some private loan scam or shady lender, had grown into a whopping $93,000 debt, incurred in the name of doing what I had been taught to believe was the right thing to do if I wanted to become successful. While I'm not here to rail against the education system or condone you bypass college or grad school just to save money, I am here to tell you that the cost-benefit analysis of earning a college or post-graduate degree in today's education system is not the slam dunk it used to be. In fact, doing so is currently on pace to become an even more dangerous gamble in the coming years.

Student debt today significantly outpaces wage growth. While median wages have increased by a mere 1.6 percent over the last twenty-five years, median debt has risen 163.8 percent. In 1990, the typical college student graduated with debt equivalent to 28.6 percent of their annual earnings. By 2015, that number had shot up to 74.3 percent. In fact, according to analysis done by the Huffington Post, student debt at graduation for the typical bachelor's degree recipient could exceed annual wages by 2023, if both figures continue to grow at the same annual rate of the last twenty-five years.

Since the recession began in December 2007, federally owned student debt has grown from 5 percent of all household debt to around 30 percent.[7] And relative to national income, student debt has more than quintupled.

But that's OK, because you'll pay your student debt back with the increased income from the job or promotion you'll get after graduation—right?

The Inevitable Automation of Jobs

What makes the burden of being saddled with crippling

student debt even worse is that some of us may be going into debt to earn degrees for career paths that may be fundamentally impacted or displaced entirely by the adoption of technology.

A research study conducted by McKinsey & Company assessed the number and types of jobs that might be created under different scenarios through 2030 and compared that to the jobs that could be lost to automation. Their key finding is that while there may be enough work to maintain full employment into 2030 under most scenarios, the transitions will almost certainly be very challenging, matching or even exceeding the scale of shifts out of agriculture and manufacturing that we've seen in the past.[8]

To put it plainly, automation will have a far-reaching impact on the global workforce. When McKinsey looked globally across all jobs, they found that a staggering 50 percent of current work activities are technically automatable by adopting currently demonstrated technology. Compounding this, a full six out of ten current occupations have more than 30 percent of their activities that are technically automatable.[9]

That means there doesn't have to be any significant advancement in technology between now and 2030 to cause more than half of our work activities to be automated to some extent.

When we consider the impact of these technologies by 2030, the jobs that could potentially be displaced by the adoption of this automation, at its midpoint, is around 400 million jobs, or about 15 percent of the global workforce. In the most aggressive scenario studied, more than 800 million global workers would have their jobs impacted by the adoption of currently demonstrated automation technology. In McKinsey's best-case scenario, less than 10 million people would have to change their occupational category.[10] But this study doesn't even attempt to account for new technology that may be developed between now and 2030.

What's more is that the current education requirements of the occupations that may grow due to the adoption of technology are higher than those roles that would be displaced by automation. In other words, the lower your education level, the more at risk your job is of being replaced by automation.

What is important to grasp from this data is the major economic impact of a relatively small increase in the adoption of today's demonstrated technology. If more than half of all occupations could have 30 percent or more of their work processes automated, how safe is your job and what can you do about it today?

Wage Stagnation

A pronounced imbalance in today's economic trends—like the stock market, corporate profits, and CEO pay—is that what is in the financial best interest of corporations is often at odds with the best interests of working-class professionals.

In June 2018, for a second month in a row, annualized inflation fully offset the average hourly wage growth of the previous year.[11] That means workers' real hourly earnings were flat over a twelve-month period, despite a falling unemployment number and historic highs in the stock market during 2018.

Investopedia defines real wage growth as the growth present after accounting for inflation. According to a recent analysis by Glassdoor, inflation generally outpaced wage growth throughout most of the country in 2017.[12] And because wage growth has remained so slow—especially in the last year or two, despite steady job growth and a strong labor market—in 2018, American workers actually felt paychecks that had fallen in real terms over the prior year.[13] As the economic recovery from the Great Recession advanced, the absence of real wage growth late in the recovery contrasted with what was happening earlier in the recovery when significantly lower inflation meant that even a modest raise afforded workers a gain in true wage growth.

In short, economic data shows that life is becoming more expensive at time when wage growth is negligible. At the same time, complexities in the global economy create historic levels of uncertainty for corporations that lead them to take a hold versus invest strategy (where companies defer hiring new employees or increasing wages until they're convinced a stable economy will last).

And then there's the politics of it all.

The Geopolitics of Jobs

In addition to technology advancements, an education system that drives us into debt without skilling us effectively for the jobs of tomorrow, and a dynamic and unpredictable global economy, there are ever-present political drivers that can fuel or hold down job growth. Historical evidence shows Western economies to be relatively cyclical. We're likely to continue to have peaks as well as valleys, booms as well as busts. Administration policies and bureaucracy will continue to impact the free markets.

A recent example of geopolitics impacting the job market is the Trump Administration's latest tariffs. Ian Shepherdson, a chief economist at Pantheon Macroeconomics, said,

> *The Administration's proposed tariffs would significantly boost core inflation. People will seek to be compensated for the squeeze on their real incomes as a result of higher prices, and their chance of being able to force their employers to pay up is better now than at any time since the crash.*[14]

If corporate profits and stock prices were near record highs at the end of 2018, yet real wage growth between 2017 and 2018 was down when tied to inflation, economists have warned that tit-for-tat tariffs could disrupt the supply chain, undermine business investment, and raise prices for consumers. This could actually wipe out the stimulus from the 1.5-trillion-dollar tax cut package that came into effect in January 2018.

In short, wages could very well rise at a faster pace in the future if the economy keeps chugging along and the labor market remains tight, but an ongoing trade war with China and even some of our allies could hurt investment spending and hold back job and wage growth.

Historically, routine political decisions have seemed inconsequential to most professionals, in part because the policies tend to change with new administrations—and because, over the past 100 years, the global workforce hasn't been negatively impacted by political decisions in a meaningful way for any significant period of time. Perhaps that's because even the most extreme external forces at work today, when taken alone, aren't significant enough to disrupt whole economies or social order.

However, we may be entering a time in which a seemingly routine political decision, or any other historically small deviation from the norm, becomes the tipping point that sends economies into chaos.

We will continue to have good times and tough times in the market, but to me the question has become one of sustainability. Are working-class professionals more negatively impacted in the downturns than they are positively impacted during the booms? I believe we're starting to see the answer become *yes*. What happens when a future recovery stalls or the status quo shifts, and the jobs that were lost simply never come back?

"Your company wants you until the day they don't."
—Julie Bauke

CHAPTER FOUR:
ARE YOU OUT-LEVERAGED?

My purpose in explaining these external forces and the impact they could have on your career is not to scare you, but rather to encourage you to assess whether you have control over your career or not. Do you have the leverage—or does your employer? Can you defend against uncertainty by taking action, or could you be wiped out by a single unforeseen decision that's out of your control?

If, after assessing your situation honestly, you realize that you don't have as much control as you'd like over your future, you've picked up the right book! Now is the time to think about what you need to be doing to regain leverage over your career and take the appropriate steps to build a life on your terms before it's too late.

If you take nothing else from this book, I want you to see your place in the world of work with your eyes wide open. Be fully aware of what's happening around you and consider the data I've presented thus far when you think about how to plan your career. If you do, you'll begin to see brand new opportunities. You'll better understand your professional vulnerabilities and learn to take stock of your individual situation to determine how to create a career on your terms moving forward.

My Inciting Incident

When I first realized I was out-leveraged by an employer, I clearly remember thinking to myself, *What am I doing? I don't like this. I'm never going get wealthy from doing it—and it could go away tomorrow.*

So this is what I did: I immediately walked away from a great corporate gig with a stable and growing company earning $190,000 per year to go out on my own and start a business from scratch.

Most people thought I was crazy.

I looked at it like this:

In order to earn the same $190,000 the following year, I would've had to maintain my book of business and grow it by 100 percent, meaning that I'd need to double the revenue to my company in order to earn the exact same amount of money. And that would only happen . . .

- IF they kept me around
- IF the compensation plan didn't change
- IF I kept the same set of accounts
- IF those accounts happened to be hiring a lot or spending a lot on recruitment advertising
- IF the economy kept plugging along
- IF I did a great job

I would've been traveling more, seeing my family less, and working harder, all for what amounted to a low financial upside with many inherent risks because the company owned all of the decisions.

I knew the business of job advertising inside and out, and the thought I had that triggered my move was this:

If I created my own company and could sell half as much as my corporate quota but keep 50 percent of it, I'd increase my income by a factor of 21x—and I'd be in control of my time, travel, and energy.

The cost? My false sense of security about having a six-figure income.

Job Security is a Myth

We've been conditioned to believe that "success" is having a steady job and spending the majority of our waking lives earning the right to pay our bills. And if the job itself happens to be a soul-sucking, horrific experience on most days, well, at least you have a job.

We respect hard work, and we admire people that "do the time" as if we're talking about a prison sentence and not a career into which we pour our heart and soul throughout the prime of our lives. It should go without saying that we all have to find ways to meet our most basic human needs, and in certain circumstances we sometimes have to do what needs to be done, despite our desires. Trust me, I've been there.

But this method of survival shouldn't become our default behavior when it comes to our vocation. Even during trying times, we should continue to learn, think, and progress into having a career that we enjoy on most days.

Don't Get Stuck with Only One Basket

We are taught in life, and especially with finances, never to put all of our eggs into one basket. If you had the foresight to buy Google stock in the '90s, after it soared you were encouraged to buy other types of stock. When you look at the allocation of investments in your IRA or your 401K, it's tied to many different types of stocks—small cap, large cap, International, and so on—to protect the principal and keep the rate of return stable and healthy.

We diversify to create protection from the unknown and to mitigate the impact of unforeseen circumstances. Yet our whole life we've been taught to follow the rules, work hard, stay the course, and things will turn out well for us. This is a mindset for my grandfather's generation—not for ours.

It's not a stretch to imagine highly motivated companies

moving to generate additional savings and boost their bottom lines by implementing automation and machine learning. It's therefore just as easy to see how the resulting negative wage growth, job displacement, a slight spike in inflation, or an uptick in the percentage of student loans that default could result in far more than 10 percent of people becoming permanently displaced or underemployed, just as they were at the peak of the Great Recession.

The Ripple Effect

Looking at the various external forces in isolation can be scary—but only to a point, because it doesn't seem plausible. It sounds like a science fiction movie.

I don't know about you, but I don't believe that robots are going to become more prevalent or more frequently seen than people during our lifetime. But it doesn't take a lot of imagination to imagine a 5 percent increase in the adoption of automation or a 3 percent increase on the default rates of student loans or a 1.5 percent increase in inflation becoming reality. The signs are all there.

If and when any of those events happen concurrently, that intersection of forces could create a catastrophe for the global workforce.

The Cost of Inaction

My question to you is this. In a world where 85 percent of working professionals are not engaged in the thing that consumes 40+ hours per week of their lives, in a world where we understand and seek out diversification and protection from the unknown, in a world where half a dozen complex external forces are capable of taking away the false sense of security that keeps people in jobs they dislike . . . Why don't we do anything about it?

Most of us justify our status quo, despite our lack of fulfillment, by holding up the tangible home or car or paycheck, no matter how average. All the while, most of us fail to properly educate ourselves and develop the skills we would need to call on if and when the stability we've relied on doesn't seem so certain any more.

And in case you're holding off, waiting for someone to sound the alarm bell and tell you, "OK, now is the time to start taking action because what's always worked probably won't work for much longer," well, I'm your whistleblower.

Today is the day to realize that you need to put in real work towards *Unboxing* the limiting beliefs you've developed about your career. Even if you love your job right now, as external forces like wage stagnation, inflation, AI and machine learning, the gig economy, and others come together, things can change. These forces are powerful individually and potentially catastrophic if they converge. They each have the opportunity to impact your industry, your company, your job . . . And if you are sitting back waiting for it to happen (or presuming it never will), you are putting your very livelihood at risk.

How many times have you turned on a football game to find a team with a big lead playing the dreaded "prevent" defense?

For non-football fans, a "prevent" defense is one in which the team without the ball keeps the other team's players in front of them in hopes that the team with the ball will not score. They bring very few pass rushers to pressure the quarterback, and they drop most of their eleven players back, trying to avoid giving up the big scoring play. As a result, yards are easier to gain and the offense tends to move quickly down field towards the opposing team's end zone. Basically, they stop playing aggressively.

More often than not, the team with the ball stays aggressive and picks up whatever yards or points that they can against this soft defense. Many times, the team playing the prevent defense is working so hard to protect their end zone—rather than playing to get the ball back as quickly as possible without giving up points or yards—that they lose, or come a lot closer to losing than they may have by sticking with the same scheme that gave them the lead in the first place.

Playing offense is always the best defense.

Now isn't the time for you to sit back in a prevent defense hoping that the final blow doesn't cross your goal line. Your place in the world, your livelihood, and your security don't have to fundamentally shift based on an external force that you can defend against if you're just informed, prepared, and committed to *Unboxing* your conditioned beliefs and building a career on your terms.

Ask yourself: *Have I been playing enough offense?*

The most common way
people give up their power
is by thinking they don't have any.
—Alice Walker

CHAPTER FIVE:
ARE YOU READY TO TAKE BACK CONTROL?

I passionately believe that we are meant to thrive, not simply survive, in our careers.

By now, you understand that there are external forces at work that make it difficult to justify putting all your eggs in the corporate basket for your entire career. You may suddenly feel part of a club knowing that 85 percent of people aren't engaged with what they do for a living either, and if you agree with Julie Bauke, you also realize that the company that pays you to do the job you don't love only wants you until the day they don't.

Given all of this, why don't more people move to create a career on their own terms? I've identified four main reasons people remain stagnant. They lack one or more of the following:

- Motivation to act
- Belief that they can succeed
- Knowledge about how to get what they want
- Knowledge about where to start

By now, you should be sufficiently motivated to act. You want to diversify to create more security and begin to thrive in a career that works for you on your terms.

If you're still on the fence, though, stop right here. I recommend that you either put this book aside and do some of your own research and reflection, or gift this book to someone that knows that they must begin to change their path and wants to learn exactly how to *Unbox* their career and build a career that allows them to live the rest of their life on their terms.

But if you're ready to take back control over your career, the next chapter will help you address number two, belief that you *can* succeed, and teach you some of mental ninja skills that the most successful people in the world use to build lives and careers they love. Then, Part II of this book will help you to fill in the knowledge gap, help you get started, and provide a tactical guide that you can use to get from where you are to where you want to be.

Let's do this!

Never take advice from people who don't know how to get where you want to go.

—Michael Hyatt

CHAPTER SIX:
MOVING BEYOND DOUBTS

If you want to stop surviving and start thriving, it's time to transform your career into something that you do on your terms, for your own reasons, while spending your time, energy, and passion on things that fire you up rather than on the things that fire up your firm's shareholders.

When you decide to take bold action and change your path, rather than stewing about your situation and doing nothing about it, you will be in the minority. You will be one of the only people in your company, among your circle of friends, and in your family that is thinking about this stuff, let alone acting on it or factoring it into your decision-making on a day-to-day basis.

Mindset for Success

In Part II, I've defined the three-step process that, when completed, will put control of your future fully back in your hands. But before we delve into the details, it is imperative that we talk about the most critical element that will set you up to be successful: your mindset.

Your mindset is what will allow you to maintain the momentum you'll build and push through the inevitable challenges that you will face getting to your goal.

You Deserve Success on Your Terms

The first thing you need to do to have any success as you move down this path is believe 100 percent in your heart of hearts that you are worthy. You are worthy of living life on your terms. You are worthy of being happy. And you can absolutely have it all.

You *can* have your life on your terms.

You *can* have an income that affords you the lifestyle that you want.

You *can* have the time and the flexibility to spend it with the people you care about, while taking care of your body, your mind, and your spirit.

As far as we know, we only get one shot at life. Continuing down a road to nowhere simply because you're already on the path, or because you've been conditioned to believe that you don't have an out, is not the way you should live.

Regardless of where you are in your career, how old you are, or the amount of money you make, you don't have to worry about waiting to "earn the right" to start taking action. Remember, you are deserving and worthy of this next level of success.

Cue the Haters

It's important to understand however, that not everyone will see it this way. People will say things like this:

"Who are you to think about doing something else?"

"You haven't even given this job a real shot yet."

"Larry over there has been here for thirty years, and he worked his way to where you want to be."

"You can't just [insert anything else you want to do instead here]!"

"You need to pay your dues just like the rest of us."

And so on . . .

Ironically, the people that will be giving you this terrible advice, or judging your actions based on their perception of what you should or shouldn't do, are usually in the exact place in their career and in their life that you never want to be.

During the time I was a collegiate and professional athlete, I had to learn the skills to become mentally tough. I had to figure out how to deal with the inevitable ups and downs of shanking the occasional punt or letting my team down or any of the dozens of things that can and will eventually go wrong for any athlete if you play long enough. I was the recipient of some amazing advice from world-class thought leaders and mentors that have become like family to me. Now it's my turn to share what I know with you so that you too can learn the mental toughness skills that will help you move down the path to building a life and career on your terms.

Emotional Mastery

Emotional mastery is a process, and it's a process that never stops. Many people spend their entire lives trying to master their own emotions—learning to pull themselves out of a funk, to let go of the things that they can't control, and so on.

Before you start your three-step journey, it's imperative that you get ALL IN on the decision you make. When Chris Dorris, the creator of the course ALL IN, is asked how to get into that state of mind, he says this:

"You simply decide."

That's it! You have the power to make a single decision that can fundamentally change the trajectory of your life. It sounds simple because it is. But that doesn't make it easy.

The Success Wheel

After you've decided to diversify your career to live life on your terms, you must declare your intentions to people and then do what it takes to get there.

Being committed to building a career on your terms and being ALL IN on that decision takes work. People will try to derail you, intentionally and unintentionally. They're tease you. You'll feel judged. At times, you may even feel like you're not ever going to get there.

I've been focused on building mental toughness skills for years, both in sports and in business, and I recently learned something about commitment that fundamentally changed how I set my goals and what I'm able to achieve. What I learned is the key to sustaining my momentum, to moving through adversity, and to letting people's negativity and hate roll off my back.

We've all committed to things that we didn't actually manifest. Think about all the New Year's resolutions you've made in the past. The many times you've claimed that you want to lose weight or get to the gym every day or change jobs or quit smoking or end a bad relationship or spend more time with your kids.

We've all been there. We've all had these moments when we started out with pure intentions and an unrivaled dedication to do what it takes. We have all been committed to making a big decision and creating a specific outcome for ourselves.

More often than not, at some point along our journey, we lose our steam. We get comfortable. We lose traction. We slip for one day, or one moment, and then we fall off the wagon. When this happens, most of us don't ever get back to the same intense level of determination and commitment that we need in order to achieve our desired outcomes. Sadly, when this happens, a lot of our goals seem to live in some type of strange dream purgatory where we're intermittently chasing the idea of the desired outcome without actually getting across the finish line.

We usually get a little bit better, at least for a time. But we never actually reach the desired outcome. What I assumed when this happened to me was that I just wasn't mentally tough enough. Something was still wrong with me, and I just wasn't as good as I used to be. Maybe I wasn't ever as good at being mentally tough as I thought I was.

But what I finally realized was that our struggles to reach big goals have everything to do, not with our ability to achieve those goals, not even with the goals themselves, but that our failures have everything to do with the nature of commitment itself.

And here's the key: the nature of commitment is that is goes away.

Let me say that again.

The nature of commitment is that it goes away.

It is therefore imperative that, as we begin this journey together, you understand the process you'll need to follow to guarantee your success. You'll have to jump on the Success Wheel:

Decide, declare, do what it takes, and recommit.

For small decisions, you may only have to recommit two, three, maybe ten times. But it will take many more recommitments to achieve something as massive as true freedom and flexibility in your career. As you get ready to tackle Step One in the next section, you'll need to learn to be unshakable in your confidence and commitment to your strategy despite the massive amount of work it will take. To overcome the pessimists in your work environment and those who will doubt, tease, and taunt you, you need to be prepared to recommit hundreds, thousands, perhaps even tens of thousands of times to get there.

Transformation

In the uncertain new world of work, if you're ever to become *Unboxed*, you must transform. You must transform how you think, what you prioritize, how you spend your time, where you invest your energy and resources, how you live your life, who you surround yourself with, and so much more. As Steve Jobs told us in 1984's famous Apple commercial, it's time to "think different." The status quo is simply untenable. The ways of the past—the social and economic contracts and the trust between employee and employer—simply no longer exist due to economic and other external forces.

It takes proper diversification, great planning, a specific but adaptable strategy (something we'll cover in Part II), and most importantly, the commitment and mindset to declare your intentions, recommit thousands of times, and move towards a life that is different from the one lived by the people you see complaining around the water cooler at the office today.

Regardless of which step you're on, you will be met with adversity. People won't get it. They'll say you're crazy, unfocused. That you're getting bad information. They'll tease you: "Why aren't you a millionaire yet?" "Why are you still coming into the office? I thought you were going to be rich by now."

These are the things you're going to hear; I know because I've heard them all. But it may surprise you that you're not only going to hear these things from strangers and people that you don't care about—you'll hear them from your friends. You may even hear them from your partner or your parents. It can be very, very difficult. Your boldness and your willingness to declare your intentions will offend people. They'll be offended by the fact that you've made a decision, that you're taking action, and that you're not afraid to tell them about it.

When this happens, here's what I want you to remember:

The world needs you to model that type of behavior. In so doing, you will inspire other people to challenge what they have been conditioned to believe about what's possible, and what they should be doing to control their own destiny.

Start with Why

Before you dedicate your journey, it's critical that you clearly define your why. *Why* are you looking to diversify and transform your career? Is it because you're unhappy and it's affecting your health? Is it because you want to set the best example for your children? Is it to allow you the flexibility to be the best partner you can be? Is it because you're now terrified of a robot takeover and want to survive?

Whatever the *why* is for you, be sure to get clear on it and then visualize what your life will be like once you've reached your goal. Will you have more money? More free time? The flexibility to finally tell your boss to shove it? The more specific your visualization is, the better.

The Power of Dedication

To help maintain discipline when you lose focus or willpower, it's important to introduce you to the power of dedication. When I decided to write this book, I dedicated the effort to my three-year-old son, the youngest of our five children. I picked him because he is the youngest, and I believe it is imperative to create a new conversation about the changes coming at us and at future generations so that we can all get better at learning how to find a vocation that allows us to be happy, earn a living, create value, and building a career worth having by following our curiosity. That is my wish for you, and it's certainly my wish for my kids when they get to adulthood and get to create their careers.

I've dedicated past goals to my wife and to my parents. I've dedicated goals to my future self—and I've even dedicated projects to my teenage self, that kid that wanted to see the adult version of me change the world ever so slightly.

I encourage you to tap into the power of dedicating your *Unboxed* transformation. You may choose to dedicate each step, specific days, a whole week, or an entire project. Whatever suits you.

Who will you dedicate your transformation to? Picture it, write it down, and declare it. This will give you the additional fuel that you will need along this journey in order to reach your target.

Hold onto Your Why

On those days when it gets tough and the haters seem to be winning, recall your visualization and how good it will feel when you are living that life. Then think about the person(s) you dedicated your transformation to. Combining these two powerful mental triggers will set you up for huge success by keeping you moving ahead, even on the days when it's the last thing you feel you can do.

Remember, you do deserve it. You can have it all. You will make it happen. Today's struggles are simply the price you must pay to earn yourself the right to live the rest of your life on your terms.

Are you ready to get started? If you are, all that's left to do is turn the page.

PART II

CREATE A CAREER ON YOUR TERMS

"We cannot solve our problems with the same thinking we used when we created them."
—Albert Einstein

THE THREE STEPS TO BUILD A CAREER ON YOUR TERMS

If the employer-employee relationship were a healthy, mutually beneficial relationship like it was fifty years ago, perhaps there would be nothing to worry about. Companies would come to you in advance of cutting your job and work with you to reskill or adapt to the jobs of the future. While there may well be some companies that take this approach and work with their employees to create a win-win in this new world of work, there will certainly be companies that do not. The recent layoffs that affected more than 14,000 employees at GM give a glimpse into how most corporations operate.[15] What happened to the GM stock price the day that General Motors slashed those jobs? It soared by nearly 8 percent![16] Investors rejoiced. Costs were slashed, productivity remained constant, and therefore profits increased—at least on a theoretical spreadsheet.

Herein lies the problem that exists: modern capitalism rewards companies that cut costs, even when revenue remains flat, because profitability increases. What's the biggest cost center in a corporation? It's employees, by a long shot—salaries, healthcare, matching contributions, and taxes.

Who really holds the cards in your career? Who has the leverage? Who is in control of your livelihood?

Understanding this cold reality, think again about 2030 and what could happen when the 50 percent of our jobs that are automatable are finally automated. If companies are able to please shareholders and increase profits by reducing their payroll expenses, why wouldn't they do it? As much as I'd love to believe morality and humanity will win the day when the time comes, it would be naïve and irresponsible not to prepare for that day the moment you understand its potential consequences. That day is today.

If we're a mere eleven years away from potential career Armageddon, it makes sense that we should be taking steps to shift the leverage from a scenario in which the company holds all the cards, to one in which we're free to live and work on what we care most about, from wherever we choose, with the people we most want to work with.

The remainder of this book will focus on three steps you must take to *Unbox* your career. I'll lay out many of the challenges and benefits of each step and give you insights into why each step is fundamental to shifting the leverage in your career from the company that employs you back to you, so that you can truly live and work on your terms.

EMPLOYER   YOU

The three steps are meant to be followed chronologically, based on where you are in your career. If you find yourself beyond Step One, feel free to move to Step Two, keeping in mind that the steps were created to provide a real-time, how-to-get-started manual. While *Unboxed* is written to be read from cover to cover, I expect and hope that, as you're moving through each step, you will come back to review and reference the material to refresh your memory and work through each step at various points during your transformation. Use this book as a reference and leverage it in any way you see fit to meet your objectives.

If you find yourself wanting (or needing) help and reassurance along the way, I'm here for you. You can find me at **www.facebook.com/coachnickmurphy**. I've also created a workbook to provide the materials you'll need in each of the three steps. You should download the workbook at **www.nickmurphy.io/unboxed-readers** before you begin the next chapter.

"The goal isn't more money.
The goal is to live life
on your terms."
—Chris Brogan

STEP ONE

PUT YOUR CORPORATE CAREER TO WORK FOR YOU

By now you may think that I'm anti-corporate career or believe that everyone should tell their boss to stick it the next time they have a bad day at work, but that's not necessarily the case. In fact, when you know how to manage your career strategically in a way that creates sustained success in the corporate world, you have a tremendous advantage over those that bypass the corporate route altogether. The key to doing so is learning how to put your career to work for you.

There is no denying the impact that sustained corporate success can have on your life. A successful corporate career can bring with it social recognition, personal satisfaction, and at least the perception of stability. More importantly, it provides you with money you can spend in any way you see fit, and knowledge and experience that can prove invaluable to you later in life as you pursue your own ventures. The successful corporate employee has more options, more time, and an easier path to diversify their career and even move out of the corporate world if they so choose.

Because so many aspects of your corporate success are out of your control, it is imperative that you **put your career to work for you rather than working for your career.** Consider new goals. Redefine how you view corporate success. It's critical that you think about how to piece together your career differently than you have been taught.

Historically, corporate success has been viewed as a ladder, implying that you must simply take the next step as you inch closer to the goal of security and retirement. A quick google search for "corporate ladder" is riddled with clip-arty looking images of professionals climbing a mountain or ascending to new heights. But today, we can no longer operate under the assumption that our trajectory is pre-determined because your ladder may very well be missing half its rungs.

Am I Ready for Step One?

Because you can't depend on the old way of succeeding at work, you are ready to begin Step One if you can relate to any of the following:

- You're feeling unfulfilled and frustrated by where you are at this point in your career

- The idea of staying in your current job for 5–10 more years makes your skin crawl, but you're not sure how to keep growing in your career

- You enjoy the office environment, but you're not progressing or learning as quickly as you'd planned

- You see the external changes that are coming and want to build a career that makes you indispensable to your (or a future) organization

Whichever your reason, you agree that what has worked for others isn't working for you, and you want to change that trajectory for the better.

Regardless of your specific situation, there are some proven strategies to build a more secure career in the corporate world and this section is dedicated to helping you discover, learn, and implement those strategies.

How to Unbox Your Corporate World

Before we try to craft the strategy that you'll use to create sustained corporate success, we need to understand why most people's strategies don't serve them well. There are three core problems with how most people plan (or don't plan!) their corporate careers.

Problem #1: We Are Reactive

Too often, we start from where we are and we react to it. It's hard to see the forest through the trees as the saying goes. But too often in our careers that metaphor feels all too close to our reality.

When we have a bad day, week, quarter, or even year in our jobs, we don't sit back and go, "Man, if I could live life on my terms, what would I be doing? What would I want to go do that I could be passionate about every day that would meet my needs and help me achieve my goals?"

Instead, we say, *I wonder which other companies are hiring for jobs like [insert your job title here]?* Therefore, it's not surprising that when we predictably find the job search process to be frustrating, many of us eventually cave in and stay where we are, accepting that a soul-sucking career is part of the human experience.

Instead of reacting to our current state, we need to start with the end in mind and work backwards. Now, it's not always possible to know exactly how your career will go, the path it's going to take, the level you'll reach, or even what industry you might end up in. But while we won't know the details of the exact path, we can and should know the lifestyle, income level, and work-life balance we hope to achieve over the course of our careers. We should also understand how much risk we're willing to accept in this pursuit.

When we're able to eliminate some of our conditioned beliefs about what's possible when it comes to changing careers, starting over, etc., suddenly the world of opportunities and solutions opens up to us.

Problem #2: Limiting Beliefs

We've been conditioned to believe that we can't have it all, so therefore we have to choose between happiness and money, independence and security, struggling to build our passions, or thriving in a cubicle.

As you undoubtedly know by now, I'm big on challenging conditioned beliefs. I completely reject the notion that we don't always maintain the right to choose what we want to be doing with our time and energy.

Every so often I run into people who prove to me that I'm right—like Goli Kalkhoran. From a young age, Goli wanted to be an attorney. She worked hard in school, earned great grades and was eventually accepted to law school at Cal Berkeley, one of the most prestigious law programs in the country. Following graduation, she took a job at a big law firm in the San Francisco Bay Area. She knew from the onset that the type of law she was practicing wasn't exactly what she wanted to be doing, but she also had student debt to get rid of. Big money was just part of the process, right?

Unsurprisingly the work didn't excite her, and after she had checked off some of her financial goals she went looking for something more appealing. She became a federal defender working exclusively on death row convictions. After her job change, she was making a bigger impact and following what she believed she was meant to do.

From the outside, she had it all—she had made it. But

inside she was miserable. Goli ultimately walked away from law altogether and started a company called Usie Booth. (Think selfies for groups at corporate and private events.) She then started an iTunes podcast with the tongue-in-cheek name *Lessons from a Quitter*.

In a recent conversation I had with her, Goli talked about the sunk cost fallacy, of which I'm a big fan. Many of us have fallen victim to the sunk cost fallacy—the idea that, because we've already come this far, we simply can't turn back. That if we have a degree in something specific, or if we spent years gaining experience, it's too late to start over. We are best served by moving around to find a better fit, and somehow, magically, someone is going to wave a magic wand and we'll be fulfilled and happy in our jobs. As nice as that would be, there is no such thing as a career fairy.

Problem #3: We Don't Live in a Vacuum

We plan our careers as if we're living them in a vacuum. Imagine your career as if you're sitting at a dinner table. But rather than choosing which table to sit at, you're told where to sit and what's on the menu. In the beginning, you're just eating the scraps—whatever comes out of the kitchen that's been left over by other patrons. After a couple years of eating these scraps, someone brings you a first-time prepared meal just for you. It's nothing great, it's essentially Spam in a bowl . . . but at least it's not leftovers.

Then a few years later somebody brings you an entire ham sandwich and maybe even garnishes it with a side salad. Your plastic fork keeps snapping in half and the food tastes like crap. But hey, its improvement. Ten years later, you get a burger with a pickle, barbecue sauce, a whole side salad, and even room-temperature french-fries. Wow, living the dream.

If we use this table as a metaphor for our careers, we're sitting in the same place, making incremental progress toward things that, in and of themselves, really aren't exciting. They're only exciting compared to how bad it's been beforehand, and how bad it would be to have nothing at all. We're in a bad place, living our careers and planning for them as if we're in a vacuum, as if our table is the only table in the only restaurant on earth.

To succeed in the corporate world today, it's imperative to expect that our priorities will evolve as we grow and move through the seasons of our lives.

The Three Seasons of Our Careers

Because we don't live or work in a vacuum, we need to anticipate, acknowledge, and accept that as our life progresses, our professional priorities will also evolve. I've worked with so many people who beat themselves up when they suddenly realize they don't love their job anymore. They blame themselves. They decide to stick it out because they've invested significant time and energy getting to this point, mistakenly assuming that their feelings of discontent are temporary lows that will eventually rebound. While this is sometimes the case, oftentimes people feeling this way are entering a new season of their career.

Season One: Early Career

This is the season in which we chase down and piece together a professional identity. In this season, we're concerned about paying our bills, having "success," proving our worth to our personal and professional contacts. The simple act of getting out on our own and being financially independent is the typical goal.

After my football career ended and I was looking for my first job outside of sports, I was willing to do nearly anything to make the transition from football to the "real world."

My goal in that season of my career was simply to check the box of having "a real job" and earning some type of income to prove to myself and my parents that I wasn't destined to be featured on some ESPN documentary about pro athletes who end up homeless.

What I lacked in experience, strategy, and know-how, I made up for in flexibility and willingness to do the work. I had almost unlimited options in terms of the kind of job I took and the size of the company I went to work for; even the location of the job didn't matter a great deal because I didn't yet have a family to support.

Fortunately, most people ultimately achieve this target

and begin feeling slightly more stable as their career begins to progress. But the satisfaction and relief we feel during our early career may not always last.

Season Two: Mid-Career

After some time and a little success, the leaves change colors and we move into the middle of our career where our goals are typically to maximize our income, grow, and try to attain a desired lifestyle. We're concerned about stagnation and limited career advancement. Suddenly work-life balance, flexibility, and being treated with respect and dignity matter a lot. We also begin to care more about impact and the meaning of our work, as well as the kinds of people we choose to work with.

Recently I started up a conversation with Emily, a Lyft driver I met in San Diego on a business trip. During the ride, I asked her if she drove full-time and if she had been driving for long (two questions I ask almost every driver I encounter). Her answer was compelling.

Emily had a traditionally successful career as an office manager. She was earning high five figures, was a respected member of her community, and was a favorite among her colleagues. One day she realized the company culture had changed over time and that she no longer enjoyed the people she worked with. She was missing after-school activities with her two young daughters and generally wasn't as fulfilled as she had once been.

She told me she had been driving full-time for about 18 months and absolutely loved the flexibility. As a driver, she could pick and choose when to work and still earn enough to support her family while maximizing her time at home.

Emily had entered a new season. She had both the self-awareness to realize her priorities had shifted and the courage to move her career in a wildly different direction.

Season Three: Late Career

Later in our careers we become more concerned with purpose and impact than ever before. We look at opportunities through a new lens. We care less about external validation and more about the quality of our lifestyle.

We set better financial goals and stash cash away so we can enjoy our life when we walk away from our career.

Far too few people plan for these changes in seasons by planning for and executing a career strategy with them in mind. Regardless of which season you're in, think back to ten years ago. What were your priorities? What were you most concerned about? What was your biggest problem? What was a busy day? What was a productive day? What made you happy? What could you never imagine doing again?

Early in my sales career as an account executive, having my own client accounts to manage and grow, along with a compensation plan I could live on was enough.

I enjoyed the challenge. I was making progress, and I got good feedback from colleagues, managers, and clients alike. Because of that, I had a lot of success inside the organization and I could hit some of my financial goals. I bought a car I was proud of, I could pay my bills every month, and I lived pretty well.

As I transitioned to the middle of my career, everything

seemed fine because I was moving up the ladder. Senior Account Executive, Major Account Executive, National Account Executive, bigger books of business, larger deal sizes, more money, more status inside the organization. Everything was "on track."

I was able to buy my first house. I could buy an even nicer car, and I didn't have to worry financially about a whole lot of things that I needed. At the time, my goals were based on tangible and financial targets. I was obsessed with how I could make more money, or how to get to a big win so I could put money away, or what to do to achieve some other arbitrary goal I had in mind.

But somewhere along the way, I realized if I stayed in the sales field that the only path forward was to move into middle management—and then, maybe if things went really well, upper management.

In both those scenarios I would have not only the problems that I faced as an account executive, but all of those problems multiplied by eight, or nine, or however big my team was. I would essentially be doing the same job from a different perspective in perpetuity. I knew almost immediately it wasn't something I wanted to do.

I remember going into interviews and being asked about what I wanted to be doing in five years. I honestly didn't have an answer because I didn't want to be in management. But I also knew it would sound bad if I said, "I just want to be crushing it in this job," or, "Honestly, I'll probably be somewhere else by then."

I also had a family by this point and didn't want to spend two to three weeks a month flying all over the country because I had some of the biggest accounts. It was no longer worth it to me to make an extra $25,000 a year if it meant spending two nights a week in a hotel room away from my kids.

But, like so many of the people I worked alongside, I didn't have anyone to tell me it was okay to look at doing something different. So every time I became unhappy, I would simply jump on a job board and look for other enterprise sales jobs. I would interview at other companies. I'd make the move, then I'd be excited for three to four months, maybe even six. But eventually the same problems I faced in the prior organization reared their heads again.

This wasn't the fault of the company. And it wasn't anything I was doing intentionally. But after two or three times, it became exhausting. I hadn't yet learned to slow down and reflect. Had I done so, I may have realized my season was changing and could've developed a more effective and specific plan to meet my new needs and regain job satisfaction.

Identify Your Season

As you begin working to shift the leverage in your career, be sure to identify which season you're in. Are you early, mid, or late career? Which are you most concerned with: maximizing income, having purpose in your work, or creating a professional identity and gaining traction for the first time?

The season you're in should dictate the types of job opportunities you're open to. I also implore you to have the foresight to know that, as you move through the seasons of your career and life, your needs and priorities will change—and therefore what's going to make you happy in your career will, too.

Don't try to create a ten- or twenty-year career plan. Create a three- to five-year plan with very specific, measurable goals to move you toward where you want to be at that point. Despite your plan, you'll have to adapt. You'll need to iterate. It won't go exactly as planned, but you'll be much better positioned to deal with the ebbs and flows of life than if you just assume everything is always going to be the same.

Sick Cycle Carousel

Like any bad habit, bad career choices tend to follow a pattern. It's not until we learn how to spot that pattern that we can change it.

Before I learned that our lives and careers are made up of various seasons, my typical job cycle used to go like this:

I would get a job at a new company and be excited about the pay bump and the new opportunity. I'd remain excited and focused for a time (usually only three to six months in my case), then I'd begin poking holes in the business, the comp plan, my boss, the market, or something else. Eventually, my frustration would win out and I saw fit to get out and go somewhere where the grass might be greener. I had opportunities, they paid more, and things were "better" overall—or so I thought.

Although the logo on my paycheck, my boss's name, and my compensation plan changed, I was basically fighting the same battles inside different organizations over and over again.

This story is not surprising when we think about it. We've learned by watching others that when we're unhappy in our job, we simply jump on a website, type in our current job title (because that's what we're "qualified" to do), check out which companies are hiring, explore how many of our arbitrary boxes this new company checks, and we jump ship to go over there.

It's been said that people don't quit their company or their job—they quit their managers. And while that's been largely true in my own experience, what I found for myself is I was actually running from the wrong problem.

It turns out I didn't hate my boss that much. It certainly wasn't that every company I worked for was terrible, although a few of them were. It wasn't even that the compensation plan was beyond repair.

My problem was that I didn't understand what I needed, what had changed, or why anything had changed in the first place. Despite my corporate moves, despite the pay increases, I wasn't getting any happier, and I wasn't putting an inch of distance between my unfulfilling career and financial or corporate job security.

How to Create Long-Term Corporate Success

It can be really overwhelming to think about your career in its entirety. A career could span fifty years in some cases. Given the seasons of our careers and all the things taking place around us, how could anyone be expected to create a career plan early on and work it to fruition throughout the entirety of their career?

Instead of thinking on such a large scale, aim to create five-year plans—short bursts of time where you can see what's coming, understand which season of your career you're in, then prioritize what you need to learn and why it matters to your overall strategy.

Start with the end in mind and then work backwards. If you're in a role where you plan on staying for five more years, where do you need to be at the end of those five years? What are the must-have skills you need to develop while you're in your current role? Who can you learn from? Who do you need to meet or work with inside the organization? Which projects can you work on to advance your career in the next five years?

When you understand what you need to have at the end of a five-year period, it's much more manageable to create a plan you can tactically and purposefully execute. Regardless of the specifics of your plan or how well it's going, always seek out learning opportunities. Constantly look around you for opportunities to learn from people who have done what you've done—or, more importantly, people who are where you aspire to be. No matter how buttoned up your plan is or how confident you are in your ability to execute it, things will change. I can't say this enough: expect to iterate and be open to change.

Smart "Job Hopping"

When you've done the work to understand what you are looking to learn, experience, or achieve in your career over the next five years, you'll be able to more clearly see whether your current role or company is best-suited to deliver that experience for you. If it's not, it's OK to consider finding a new firm no matter how long you've been employed there.

Things have changed drastically since my grandfather's forty-one years at the same insurance company. Today, there is data to support that the once frowned upon notion of routinely moving around from company to company can more quickly enable you to climb the corporate ladder, earn promotions, and increase your total compensation more rapidly.

According to the Federal Reserve of Atlanta, "job hopping" can almost double your salary increase when compared to staying inside your existing organization.[17] In fact, the last time sticking around netted higher wage growth than changing jobs was in 2011. This data suggests that job hopping isn't necessarily just a short-term win, but it can be a good strategy to maximize your long-term salary, too. I've long been a proponent of this strategy and it was one I utilized in my corporate career.

When I worked in the advertising industry, I moved around every two to three years. This wasn't necessarily my plan from the outset, and as we discussed in a previous section, I didn't always move for the right reasons. However, by being open to changing jobs I saw opportunities arise more frequently than I anticipated, and as a result I saw my base salary go from $36,000 to $110,000 between 2010 and 2015. This, of course, doesn't account for sales commissions and total compensation, which largely followed the same trajectory. My point here is simply to show the dramatic increase in guaranteed earnings you can attain from being open to changing companies when you follow your plan.

When we earn more money, we have more options.

This isn't rocket science. We can save more, pay off debt faster, and invest more in things we care about—retirement, a side hustle, vacations, investment properties, stocks, etc.

Although I significantly increased my earnings by moving around frequently in the corporate world, what I ultimately found is it didn't solve any of my underlying problems or unhappiness. The higher-paying job could still go away at a moment's notice, and I'd be searching for my next job with what amounted to a higher cost of living due to lifestyle improvements.

If It's Broke, Fix It

If 30 percent of corporate jobs will be 50 percent automatable by the year 2030, we'd be wise to begin learning the skills of the future today. Of course, this is easier said than done, because no one has a crystal ball—but there are lots of ways to learn new skills and diversify your abilities.

There's a saying in the NFL, "The more you can do," implying that if everything else is equal, the guy who can play a position and also go down on special teams and make plays is more valuable than the guy who only plays one position. That's long been a key to making and staying on an NFL roster, and the principle applies to careers outside of sports as well.

Take a high-level look at your industry and identify skills you believe will be relevant, skills you're curious about, and find places to educate yourself on those skills. Think outside the box on where to get this education. You do not necessarily need to go back to school or earn a new (and expensive) degree to learn the skills of tomorrow. There are plenty of free or nearly-free places online where you can learn just about any skill under the sun from the comfort of your own home. Some of my favorite resources for learning are webinars, blogs, podcasts, YouTube, and online courses.

Whether you're building new skills for far into the future or for the next five-year section of your career plan, make sure to always be learning. You don't need to wait for doomsday to start taking what you've learned and moving forward.

Take Bold Action

Kristina decided early in her career that she wanted to be a VP of sales by the age of 30. Talk about ambitious! She was hired on at a growing advertising company after graduating from college, where she quickly built a reputation as a high performer through her dedication, work ethic, and laser focus on knowing her clients and crushing her quota.

After only a few short years, she was preparing for an upcoming interview regarding a promotion to National Account Executive. Around the same time Kristina was preparing for this huge new opportunity inside her company, a recruiter from a competitor reached out and wanted to know if she would be interested in coming over to work for them. The internal promotion was not by any means guaranteed yet, but the new company wanted her to come over in a lateral move with roughly the equivalent job title and salary range.

After further discussion and delays in the promotion timeline, she agreed that it might be in her best interest to "take a chance" and consider a move to a different organization all the way across the country. She took the interview and ended up earning the job. Within six months at her new company she was promoted to National Account Executive, and before long was leading her region in sales.

The compensation plan at her new company was structured as salary plus commission with a small amount of equity that vested after a set period of time if she was still at the firm. At the onset, her decision to change jobs could have been perceived as a lateral move with potential upside—certainly no guarantee. However, not long ago her new company was acquired for more than a billion dollars and Kristina was able to cash in on the equity. While her shares were minimal compared to more senior, tenured colleagues, her calculated risk certainly paid off, both with extra cash and the corresponding experience of growing with a company through a major acquisition—a huge resumé booster.

Shortly after the acquisition I called to congratulate her. I said, "Well, now that you have a little extra cash in your pocket you can afford to go be a VP of Sales at a start-up and check that VP goal off!"

She replied, "Based on what I've seen, I don't think I want to be a VP of Sales anymore."

Post-acquisition, Kristina relocated back to California with her new husband, who she met in her new city only after taking the job with the competitor. Today, despite how well things turned out professionally, she admits that her now-husband is her most significant prize for her willingness to take strategic risks.

Kristina's story illustrates not only the value of moving around and the upside to taking risks, but also how our paths can change when we're open to opportunities. Goals we've held onto for years sometimes move away as we gain perspective and shift into a new season in our careers and lives.

Don't Wait for Proof

My good friend and mentor Chris Dorris has often shared a story about his nephew Benny. A few winters ago, Chris took a trip back east to visit family. When he walked into his brother's house, he tossed his keys up on the mantel underneath the flat-screen television and sat down in his favorite recliner to enjoy time with the family.

Benny, barely old enough to crawl, started moving towards them, cooing and making all of those baby sounds we're so familiar with but can't understand. Benny didn't hesitate; he kept crawling but no one really knew what he was doing. Eventually, Chris realized Benny must have spotted his keys on top of the mantel and was intent on getting them, despite his obvious limitations.

Now Benny couldn't even stand. Here was a toddler with no ability to communicate what he wanted, no physical ability to get the keys himself, and yet he was 100 percent committed to figuring out how to get those keys. In fact, he wasn't thinking about his obvious limitations at all. He was on a mission, and in his mind the outcome was guaranteed. Benny was going for it even if his goal was completely impossible on the surface.

After watching in amazement, Chris stood up, walked to the mantel and said, "Oh, Benny, do you want these keys?" Benny cooed and reached. Chris then pulled the keys down and handed them to his nephew. This child, who had absolutely no business thinking he could get the keys off the six-foot-tall mantel didn't stop to say, "Well, you know, I can't really stand, and I don't have the ability to ask for what I want, so I'll just sit here knowing I can't have the keys." He took immediate action and he manifested his desires by moving towards what he wanted, even when it was impossible.

Regardless of where you are in your professional journey, or how happy or unhappy you may be, it's imperative that we challenge our conditioned beliefs and understand we always have the option to choose, that taking action is the only thing that's going to change our current situation.

It's typically after this action that we understand how things play out. As Steve Jobs used to say, we can't connect the dots forward but we can connect them backward. Too often we remain in our comfort zone, assuming we can't have something different because we're too far along or we don't know exactly how we'll reach our goal—but these are not good reasons to stay put.

Whether you're happy in your current job now, or you're moving into a new season soon, realize your priorities and needs are going to change. Always start with the end in mind and make sure you are making decisions based on where you want to be in a handful of years.

Get Better at Asking for Specific Help

Once you know *exactly* what you want, it is critical that you are very specific in your asks when you are looking for help from your network. Too often we say things like, "If you know of anyone hiring, please let me know," assuming it will be enough. And it's not. People simply don't know what to do with that. If you've decided you want to start looking for something different or you're ready to take the next step in your corporate journey, you must be able to coach your team of influencers on *exactly* what you're looking for and *specifically* how they can help you.

Knowing what to ask for and how to make that ask is great, and really important. But what do you do if there aren't a lot of decision makers in your immediate network?

How to Attract Career Influencers

Think outside the box when you're looking for people you know who may be able to help you land your next corporate gig or promotion. Too often, when we think about our networks, we focus only on the people we believe are in a position to make a decision to get us what we want right now, significantly limiting the people we discuss our ambitions with. Filtering your contacts in this way puts you at a massive disadvantage and lessens the likelihood of finding a job through your immediate network.

Putting aside the fact that you may not have built up the relationship to earn you the right to ask that person to hire you, or encourage them to ask someone below them on the org chart to hire you, there are far more effective ways to network your way to a decision maker.

At one time, I became bored with the recruitment advertising industry and wanted to get out. After spending several years at three of the world's largest job sites, I was simply burned out.

After a lot of painful soul-searching, I decided I wanted to pursue a new industry: software sales. I had friends "killing it" in software sales, making three times what I was with half the clients to manage. There seemed to be more money in a less commoditized industry, so I decided to take a crack at landing that type of job.

After a dozen failed attempts applying into the black hole of online job sites, I finally received some great advice from renowned career coach Julie Bauke. Julie's advice was to rethink how I approached my search and look to people I knew that may have a connection to someone in a position to interview and ultimately hire me.

That golden piece of advice led me to find trusted people in my network, people who cared about me and would go the extra mile to think through who they knew that might be able to help me.

Once you're able to be specific about what type of job, skill, or promotion you want to go after, think about who you know in your network who might have a connection with someone who can help you. Notice that I *did not* say "think about who you know in your network that *can hire you.*"

The Power of Referrals

Prior to getting Julie's great advice, I would find myself sifting through my 2,500+ LinkedIn contacts, looking only for people who had titles of "Director" or "Recruiter" inside one of the large software companies I was interested in. I would just ping them out of the blue with my resumé and a blurb about how great I would be if I worked there. I later realized that by employing these tactics, I sounded exactly like the hundreds of other candidates trying to get the attention of these same executives and recruiters every single day. I was just another annoying piece of noise to them, and regardless of my intentions and efforts, my tactics were fundamentally flawed.

Implementing Julie's advice, I reached out to a handful of trusted contacts with a very specific ask. One of the people I contacted was my sports psychologist when I was in college. I knew him and trusted him but had no idea if he'd be able to help me or not.

As it turns out, since his days helping me master mental toughness in my sports career he had become a well-sought-after corporate speaker and coach and was currently under contract with several large software companies as both a keynote speaker and a coach to their executive teams.

In less than a week, I had phone interviews at Oracle, Salesforce, CA, and a handful of other large software companies in the Human Capital Management space. This was all due to a person I never would have gone to had it not been for Julie's advice to think about who would be willing to go the extra mile for me.

Here's a copy of the actual email he sent on my behalf to a VP-level contact at Salesforce:

> *Hey man, I want to introduce you to someone, he's a badass like you, just a little younger. A great friend and former client of mine, Nick Murphy is looking for a new opportunity. He's currently at*
> _____.
>
> *I coached him when he was playing in the NFL, he's*

a class act, and I'm more than comfortable recommending him. I've pasted below what he said he's looking for so if you have any ideas for Nick please let him know, as I've copied him on this email.

"I'm currently looking for SaaS, HCM, or big data sales opportunities on the West Coast, So Cal, or AZ ideally, but I'll consider the Bay Area for the right fit as well."

Thanks Larry — CD

It's pretty awesome when you earn an email like this from a contact in your network, but it was after this email introduction that all the magic happened. Below is the actual email Larry CC'd me on less than twelve hours later.

Thanks CD, Nick good to meet you here. I'll ask our recruiter to reach out to get you into the process, his name is Don B. Ping me if you don't hear back within the next few days. Best — Larry

I mean, WOW! The amount of time (and luck) it would

have taken to get into that company's process had I done it the "traditional way" is something I don't even want to think about. I was able to interview with Oracle and two other software companies in this same way.

Eventually I decided through the interview process that, while they were all great opportunities, I simply didn't want to work at a huge company after all. I wanted to have a more direct impact on mission, revenue, and really carve a path forward to skip mid-management and get closer to strategy.

I ultimately determined that this path I sought didn't exist for someone who hadn't checked the management boxes, but going through this exact process led me to go back out on my own and begin working on everything I'm doing today.

I tell you all this not to give you a life story or insist to you that it needs to be done exactly this way, but rather to illustrate that, by doing things differently, taking good advice, and implementing it, the outcomes can be drastic—and fast.

Give Yourself Some Grace

The final piece of advice I'll leave you with as you work through Step One is to simply be patient with yourself and forgive yourself when things get hard. It's natural and normal to feel lost, stuck, frustrated, and even hopeless.

Be aware of when you're chasing your tail or some new shiny object. Whether it's a new logo, boss, or bump in pay, if you haven't identified your season, gotten clear on your 3–5 year plan, solved for what you want and need during this season, and clearly articulated it to your network of influencers, you're likely to end up with the same problems you face today.

Work hard at honing the self-awareness to understand when you're aspiring to live like Bill Murray's character in the movie *Groundhog Day*, where you're doing the same thing, day in and day out, never really changing the end result.

Take a step back and think, *How do I most profoundly want to use the rest of my career, and what do I need in this season, this role, or this company that can help get me there?*

And then act. Even a very small action is exponentially more powerful than staying in your status quo and complaining, or stewing over all the things you're not getting.

Your corporate job is a part of your journey. It's not the destination, but rather a vehicle to help you learn the skills, build the network, and earn the money you need to build a stable life.

Once you have put your corporate job to work for you, you're ready to take Step Two in your journey.

"There are no downsides to a side hustle. There are only benefits to building more than one source of income."

–Forbes

STEP TWO

DIVERSIFY BY CREATING A SIDE HUSTLE

There is a lot of buzz out there around creating a "side hustle." A side hustle simply means creating a business, or some additional source of revenue on your own, while maintaining your primary source of income, like a corporate job. Side hustles can vary from 1-to-1 services like coaching, to something like drop-shipping where the business owner never touches a product, never meets the buyer, and can operate from anywhere in the world, at any time of day.

Side hustles are becoming more and more popular thanks to shows like ABC's *Shark Tank* and social media entrepreneur stars like Gary Vaynerchuk who have made it sexy to be an entrepreneur. Of course, almost anyone would agree that the idea of having an income you can make passively, or on your own, outside of your primary job is a great idea. But before we go any further, let's talk about how to know if you're ready to build your side hustle.

You're Ready to Create a Side Hustle If:

- You've completed Step One and are making your corporate career work for you

- You want to protect against the uncertainty of a single source of income by creating diversification from a separate income stream

- You're an entrepreneurial-minded corporate employee who has an idea you want to test before jumping out to run a company full-time

- You want to scratch your entrepreneurial itch and try something new, but you don't have a lot of time or resources to pour into scaling a business full-time from day one

- You're an opportunistic individual who understands how other people are making money and want a piece of it for yourself

- You're a risk-averse entrepreneur who wants to try something for the first time, but can't quite justify going all in on starting and running a business without some proof it'll work

- You're a planner: you know that by a certain date, or at some point in the near future, you will walk away from your job and create an income stream to help bridge the gap between now and what's next.

Creating a side hustle may be right for any self-motivated person who just wants more than their current career has to offer. Maybe you already have a degree or specialized training in your field and you view that investment of time and education in your career as something you don't just want to quit doing. Maybe you don't necessarily dislike what you do but your career has plateaued and you want something more. Perhaps you need a creative outlet, or you want to improve your personal brand or add to a new skill set. Maybe you want a hobby that pays for itself—or you just don't feel like you're operating near your full potential or sufficiently hedging your success.

Regardless of your reasons or situation, the best part about a side hustle is that anyone with the right mindset and drive can create one. For most of the side hustlers I've coached or consulted with, the most paralyzing aspect of creating something new is simply knowing where to begin. Step Two is dedicated to helping you do just that.

Goal and Purpose

Most people believe that to create a side hustle they

must have a great idea and understand exactly how to do it. I completely disagree. There are only two absolute requirements for an aspiring side hustler to have: a goal and a purpose.

Before you start worrying about what your idea is and how you're going to execute it, or you start poking holes in all the things you don't know yet, think about why you want a side hustle in the first place. Quantify "why" in terms of dollars and time. A side hustle is not a hobby. A side hustle is also not a full-time business that needs to scale to an acquisition or an exit from the onset. However, it *is* a business, and every business must generate revenue. Therefore, your side hustle journey must begin by defining a financial target.

Do you want to earn an extra $5,000 per month to pay off your soul-sucking student loan? How about an extra $1,500 per month to justify that new Tesla you keep dreaming about? Perhaps you're looking to earn $1,000,000 over the next three years so you can walk away from your job, debt-free, with cash in the bank.

Once you have your financial target locked in, be sure

to take time to consider and expand upon your "why." Perhaps you selected your financial goal to take your family on an annual vacation and spend more quality time together, perhaps it's to afford a larger home so you can host family events, or maybe it's simply because you want to prove to yourself—or someone else—that you can.

Whatever your purpose, don't continue reading until you can fill out the statement of commitment and get excited about it when you re-read it:

STATEMENT OF COMMITMENT

I, _____,

WILL GENERATE $_____ BY _____

SO I CAN _____.

This exercise will help you clarify your "why" and commit to your financial goal, as well as put a timeline in place. Once you've created your financial target and have a good idea of what you're trying to achieve through your side hustle, now it's time to get clear on your concept.

Which Camp Are You In?

When it comes to choosing an idea for your side hustle, you're probably in one of these three camps:

- The person with absolutely no idea where to start
- The person who has multiple ideas and can't land on which one to execute
- The person who knows exactly what they want to do and just needs to know where and how to start

The Person with No Idea

Many people assume that if you haven't come up with a groundbreaking business idea or aren't clear on how you're going to reach the goal you just set that there is absolutely no way to get there—and that's simply not true. There are plenty of ideas that are proven to work as side hustles and full-time businesses alike.

Below is a short list of proven side hustle ideas. This list certainly is not all-inclusive, and it's not as if you need to choose one of these for your side hustle. These are simply examples of proven concepts to help you start brainstorming.

- Create an Etsy store
- Manage social media for a small business
- Teach your expertise via an online course
- Become a virtual assistant
- Open a drop-shipping business
- Give music lessons

A Few Inspirational Success Stories

Brian Thompson, a copywriter and creative director, launched a website on April Fool's Day in 2014 offering to put tweets on physical artwork. The venture quickly turned from a joke into a lucrative side hustle. Thompson now sells tweet art at Permanent140.com and offers custom laser engraving at LasersMakeItAwesome.com. His creations bring in around $1,500 a month.

Daniel Grove combined his love of science fiction and photography to offer fun portrait sessions for lovers of *Star Wars*, *Harry Potter*, and other sci-fi favorites. While the Texan has expanded his services to include wedding and family photography, he began by specializing in cosplay photography. Grove earns an average of $1,600 a month and still maintains his day job.

David Gaylord and two of his friends each invested just $250 of their own cash in 2015 to launch Bushbalm, a skincare company that creates essential oil blends to soothe skin, prevent ingrown hairs, and reduce redness on sensitive areas of the body. The business now brings in around $2,500 a month.

And my personal favorite . . .

Jill Bong's pet chicken, Speck, died from a mating injury in 2011, a common occurrence among domestic chickens that can be prevented if the chicken is wearing a vest, or saddle. About a year later, Bong, an engineer in Colorado, launched Chicken Armor, which produces low-cost, low-maintenance saddles for farmers all over the world. Bong brings home an average of $1,500 a month from her business. Seriously.

As you can see, the possibilities are nearly endless.[18] However, here are the most critical things to consider as you get closer to choosing a course of action:

- How much time am I willing and able to put into my side hustle business at the beginning? after a few months? long-term?

- How much extra money do I have to infuse into my side hustle? zero dollars? a couple hundred dollars? a thousand dollars or more?

- What am I qualified to do? This question primarily revolves around people considering a side hustle in the services industry. Think resumé writing, life coaching, etc. Things like this require an experience or a perspective that resonates with a certain type of person to help create value in their life.

- What am I most interested in? Follow your curiosity. The Internet is an amazing place, and it allows for people to make money in businesses in which they may have no expertise—i.e. drop-shipping.

The Person Who Has Too Many Ideas

Early in my entrepreneurial career, and even today, having enough ideas was never my problem. What I struggled with early on was with execution, making good decisions, and being efficient with both time and resources.

In my experience, the entrepreneurial-minded person with too many ideas (there's no such thing as too many ideas, by the way) doesn't have a problem coming up with what they could do. They simply need to know how to start, where they're going, and how to get there. These people are typically opportunistic and have the unique ability to think around an opportunity or a problem and find the path of least resistance.

If this is you, we just need to point you in the right direction. Take some time now to map out all your ideas, no matter how crazy or out of reach they may seem at the moment, and flush them onto paper to create a list of possible opportunities. Take your time with this and be sure to get *all* of your ideas out on paper.

Note: while there is no hard and fast rule about side hustles—and there are plenty of people who run multiple businesses successfully at the same time—if you're just getting started and keeping your day job, I highly encourage you not to launch multiple side hustles if this is your first time creating a business of your own.

Once you've successfully gotten every one of your ideas

out on paper, it's time to narrow your ideas down to three. To do this, read each one and ask yourself:

- Will I be passionate about this long-term?
- Do I have the skills or knowledge to pull it off?
- Does it align with my purpose?
- Can it meet my financial goal?

Using these questions as a filter, narrow down your list. Once you have a list of three, take some time away and think long and hard about which one excites you the most. Which one do you see as the best opportunity? Which one will you be passionate about and enjoy long-term? Which one creates impact and adds value to the people you care about? Which one gets you to your financial goal both safely and quickly? Which one are you curious enough about to throw yourself into every day, especially on the tough days?

The Person Who Knows Exactly What They Want to Do

If you're the person who knows exactly what they want to do in their side hustle, my immediate question for you is, "What have you been waiting for?"

It's likely you have been waiting for proof that you know how to execute your idea successfully. This ties back to the importance of mindset and why we should never wait for proof. No one was ever a successful entrepreneur until they were. No one was ever a professional athlete until they were. No one was ever a CEO until they were. Don't wait for proof.

Regardless of how certain you are about your idea, I still recommend that you work through the exercises in the prior two sections to make absolutely certain you are dead set on your direction and that it aligns with the goal and purpose you set in your commitment statement at the beginning of this section. Nothing is worse than having the greatest idea of all time, beginning to execute and build that thing, only to realize halfway down the path that your priorities have shifted or you've changed your mind about what a great idea it was in the beginning.

Mastering Your Elevator Pitch

Now that you're clear on your idea, it's time to describe your business concept. Someone who can quickly, simply, and powerfully describe their business is said to have a great "elevator pitch." The term describes the ability to share what your business does in the time it takes to ride on an elevator with a stranger. The goal is to explain it in a way that leads someone to ask more questions, want to talk with you further, or—at the most basic level—clearly understand what it is you do.

Despite how simple it sounds, getting good at describing your business concept is half art, half science, plus a lot of practice. While you may feel like you're already able to do this because you just finalized your idea and have gone through the exercises in the previous section, it will almost always take more practice and reworking than you think.

Your elevator pitch must do the following:

- Clearly describe the problem you solve
- Get your ideal customer to care
- Pique curiosity and lead to a "tell me more" type of response

If your pitch fails to achieve all three items, you haven't found your pitch yet. Keep working at it.

Practice, practice, practice. It's extremely important that you practice your elevator pitch in your head, then out loud, and then use it on potential customers or even strangers that you run into.

Pro Tip: call and leave yourself a voicemail giving your elevator pitch, then go back and listen to it. There's something about hearing yourself recite your pitch that leads you to make changes and then reinforce the final version in your mind.

Your Market Position

Once you've identified your goals, honed your idea, and can describe your business concept, it's time to identify your strategic position in the market. In business school, students are taught to perform a SWOT analysis on their business ideas: Strengths, Weaknesses, Opportunities, and Threats. While going through a formal SWOT analysis in every instance can be overkill, it is a helpful exercise for the first-time side hustler to complete as it can help clearly map out your market position in a way that's simple to digest.

The SWOT analysis is comprised of four quadrants, with strengths and weaknesses on the top left and top right, and opportunities and threats on the bottom left and the bottom right, respectively.

Following the sample in your workbook, think through your business's strengths, weaknesses, opportunities, and threats. While completing your analysis, it's incredibly important to be honest with yourself. Typically, if you find your analysis has all strengths and opportunities and you can't think of more than one weakness or one threat, you need to think longer and harder about the reality of your business idea. The same is true if you have too many negatives. A good analysis is typically quite balanced, without any quadrant containing significantly more items than others.

Once you've completed your SWOT analysis, take a minute and go back to your initial goal, purpose, and timeline to make sure everything aligns. If it does, you have the proper clarity to begin moving ahead.

It's imperative to align your SWOT analysis with your stated financial goal and purpose. If your stated goal is to make an extra $100 a week, maybe your side hustle is to become the go-to dog walker in your neighborhood. If your goal is to make $5,000 or $10,000 a month, then you may need to spend more time on the SWOT analysis.

This part of the process can feel a little overwhelming if it's your first time going through a SWOT exercise, but don't fall victim to paralysis by analysis. It's not necessary to overthink every little detail. It's completely okay not to have all the answers or predict the exact path forward. No entrepreneur or side hustler ever has every answer, and there will always be changes that cause you to adapt, pivot, and revise your strategy as you move through it, no matter how perfect your pre-launch plan may be. The SWOT exercise is there to help you see the full picture and determine how to deploy resources, what to build first, and assist you in getting ahead of potential pitfalls.

Time to Check In

Here's what you should have buttoned up at this stage:

- Commitment statement completed
- Business idea selected
- Concise, accurate description of your business concept with a good elevator pitch
- Understanding of both the SWOT analysis and your strategic position in your given market

Become an Industry Expert

By now, you have a direction that you're confident in and hopefully excited about. The next step in your side hustle journey is to become an expert in your chosen industry. Depending on your background and the idea you choose, you may already be very knowledgeable. But, whether you're an expert or not, there are two sides to every equation, and I want to present you with the two most critical elements you'll need to become an expert."

The Buyer Persona

A buyer persona, sometimes referred to as a customer avatar, is defined as a semi-fictional representation of your ideal customer based on market research and real customer data. At this stage, you probably don't have any existing customers, so your persona is likely to adapt as you acquire them. However, in its simplest terms, creating a buyer persona is simply giving a name and a face to your target customer.

It's important that your persona is based on data and not gut feel. Buyer personas have replaced demographics in the minds of marketers and sophisticated entrepreneurs because, when done correctly, the work you put into identifying your buyer persona will inform your brand, messaging, pricing, and so much more about your business.

Today's buyer persona isn't simply about vague or general demographics. Your persona (or personas—it's OK to have more than one) will include your target buyer's age, occupation, education, and even their personality. Are they married or not? What are they motivated by? What are they afraid of? What are their frustrations?

Where do they hang out online? Who influences them and their decisions? How much money do they make? And more.

To save you a ton of time and frustration on thinking about everything important that could be included in a persona, I've created a persona template and included it in your workbook. This persona is the same one I use when building new strategies and companies today.

Your Target Market

Now it's time to research your ideal customer so you can accurately fill out your buyer persona template. Here are some places to begin looking for this information.

Facebook groups. These days, there's a group for just about everything. By joining groups related to your business, you'll hear feedback, complaints, and ideas, and you'll likely discover other resources that are shared among members.

LinkedIn. Go look at the profiles of people you believe represent your buyer persona. There are two highly valuable sections of a LinkedIn profile I want you to focus on:

- "People also viewed"—located in the right sidebar as you scroll down the profile (not all users have this enabled, so if you don't see it, simply find a different profile)
- "Interests"—near the bottom of most profiles

Be careful not to go down the rabbit hole of following these links all over LinkedIn. Instead, look for trends. If you sell to marketers, for example, do many of them attend a specific industry conference? Do they belong to a specific association? Is there a LinkedIn group that many of them share? If so, it may be worth attending or joining.

Your network. Talk to people and interview them about their experience with the problem you're looking to solve. Anyone who has shared their frustration in the past, anyone who is using a competitor's solution (more on this in the next section), plus your own personal experience are all invaluable places to get meaningful data about your persona(s). Do not overlook or discount these resources as you build your buyer personas.

Now that you have the tools to build your buyer persona, it's time to go get it done! When you're finished, you'll be ready to learn about the other side of the equation: your competition.

Understanding Your Competition

Note this section is called "*understanding* your competition," not "*identifying* your competition." You've already identified your strategic market position and completed your SWOT analysis so you can point out who your competitors are. This section is built to help you learn everything you can about how they run their business and how they're positioning themselves to your target customers.

Not too long ago, our dishwasher broke and my wife wanted me to fix it. (By the way, fixing things is something I simply cannot do. I have zero patience.) Despite that reality, I was going to try.

Once I identified the part I needed, it was time to

decide where I could go to get that part. It turned out both Home Depot and Lowe's carry the part, and they're each about two miles from our home in opposite directions.

Alternatively, I could have decided (either before or during the repair process) that it would just be easier or cheaper to buy a new appliance. In that case, I would likely choose between Costco and Best Buy.

I also weighed the option to call a repair service so someone else could fix it for me, in which case I would turn to Google to search for someone local who was qualified to help solve my problem. If the repairman identified a new issue or otherwise redefined my problem during his inspection, I'd then be choosing between getting a second opinion and authorizing the newly defined repair from the service tech already in my home.

In the end, I called the repair service, because, well, I can't fix anything!

My point, besides letting you know that I'm the least "handy" man in the world, is simply to point out that there are multiple ways to think about a problem from the perspective of your potential customer. Try to put yourself inside the problem from their perspective. Be sure to consider where they are, what they're facing, and ALL of the potential options they can consider to reach their desired outcome. It's by thinking about your competition in this way that you will best position your side hustle for quicker success.

Lowe's may not consider Costco their competitor. After all, Lowe's primarily sells parts, and Costco sells, well, everything. But by brainstorming your indirect and direct competitors you will have flushed out not only clear competitors, but also some not-so-obvious ones that you'll want to pay attention to.

There are two types of competitors to be aware of:

- *Direct competition*—businesses that sell the same, or essentially the same, products or services
- *Indirect competition*—businesses whose products or services are not the same but that could satisfy the same consumer need

Tools to Track Your Competitors

Once you know who your competitors are, there are some interesting ways to make sure you understand what they're doing and how they're positioning themselves to your target buyers. One of the most popular tools to help you keep up on competitors is to set up Google Alerts. To do this, simply go to google.com/alerts and fill out the information in the form—in this case, your competitor name or product you want to track. Click "create alert," and you'll begin receiving real-time updates of your competitor's promotions, sales, and other offers.

Another useful tool for tracking your competition is called Social Mention. Social Mention is very similar to Google Alerts, but it's solely for social media. Essentially, the tool provides you with a list of mentions of your competition across social media platforms. Social Mention monitors over 100 sites, including Facebook, Twitter, YouTube, and Google.

One of my favorite tools is called the Wayback Machine. It's an Internet archive where you can view the history and evolution of any website or web page from 1996 through today. This is particularly helpful for the side hustler who wants to see where their competitors were when they were getting started. At the time of writing, the Wayback Machine archives more than 345 billion web pages.

Pro Tip: If you're looking for a little extra inspiration, go back and look at Amazon.com in 1999 to see what's possible for you in your business.

These are just a couple examples of the dozens of helpful tools available to you. I've included a number of them in your workbook.

Don't Be Discouraged

The purpose of going through these competition exercises is to help you understand the ways in which you can compete with your competitors for customers or users. If you find yourself feeling insecure, questioning, or doubting yourself after this exercise, congratulations! You've reached the very first time you're going to have to recommit to your side hustle. Business is a lot like life, and no matter what business you're in, there will always be someone with more money, a faster website, more customers, better reviews, more follows, etc.

Fixating on these things and chasing your tail is a fool's errand and a waste of your valuable energy. Focus on what you can control.

You don't need to go crazy here. Simply do enough work in this section to understand who your competitors are, how they position themselves to your target persona(s), where your side hustle fits into the market, and come up with two or three initial ideas about where you have an opportunity to come in and compete for their business. Once you've done that, it's time to move on.

Marketing and Sales Strategies

Congratulations on getting this far. Most people who aspire to create a business on the side or differentiate their income through a side hustle fall off the wagon somewhere between ideation and where you are right now. Take a quick moment and give yourself a little love for how far you've come and how much closer you are to hitting your goals!

By now, you should have a clear foundation in place, you know everything there is to know about your target market and buyer persona(s), and you have your product or service ready to go. Now it's time to think about how to sell it: how to get your product or service in front of as many target buyers as humanly possible in the shortest amount of time, with limited resources, for as little cost as possible.

THE CUSTOMER JOURNEY

The first thing to do is identify the best marketing and sales strategies for your business. There are five primary categories that your strategy will fall into, aligning with your buyer persona's customer journey. We'll go through all five in some detail here, noting that most businesses will eventually have marketing or sales efforts across all five categories.

Organic Traffic

The term *organic* refers to creating content that allows your customers to find your business and engage with you over time. The organic strategy you may be most familiar with is SEO (search engine optimization). If you're building a personal brand to create a coaching business, for example, it will be important that you create content in the form of blog posts or podcasts so your expertise on your topic is out there on the Internet for search engines to find. That way when people are searching online for something you offer, they'll have the opportunity to come across your content, realize your expertise, and engage with your brand. When you do so, there is the potential for those internet searchers to turn into leads, prospects, and ultimately sales.

Organic traffic is a double-edged sword. It's far and away the cheapest of the five strategies because it's basically free. If you have an optimized website that Google can crawl, then you don't need to worry about doing much else to have the *potential* for showing up in search results. Your content will be indexed and the opportunity for it to be discovered on the Internet is there. The downside, of course, is that it's a very, very slow process, and having an optimized website doesn't guarantee you free visibility from search engines. SEO offers a disproportionate reward for those who show consistency over time.

But let's get tactical for a second. If you calculate that your side hustle needs to attract ten potential clients to close $1000 in new business in your first month to be successful, relying on organic traffic simply isn't the strategy that will deliver those immediate results for you. This does not mean you should discount its long-term value or abandon this strategy altogether; it simply means if you're trying to turn strangers into prospects, customers, and revenue quickly, organic traffic is not likely to achieve that initial goal for you.

Note: the amount of content you create, where you place it, how it's structured, and the frequency of your posts will all significantly impact how well your content is indexed by search engines and available to be discovered online.

Warning: don't get sucked too far down the content marketing and SEO optimization rabbit hole at this stage of the game. Both areas are complex, detailed, and changing constantly.

Paid Ads

Paid advertising can be extremely effective because you're reaching people who are further along in the customer journey and ready to buy or acquire what you have to offer. By now, most of us have purchased something that we were originally exposed to through a paid ad.

Providing your email address in exchange for a free report, "liking" a sponsored Facebook page, following an Instagram account after viewing their sponsored post, downloading a new app, or creating a free account on a new website are all examples of actions users can take in response to paid ads.

Homework: think about the actions you want your buyer persona to take with your content or paid ads. Then, jot down your initial ideas, even if you're not ready to spend anything on paid advertising right away. This will help inform the types of content you create and drive the behaviors from your personas that are most likely to help you meet or exceed your goals.

Some of the most popular paid channels are Google AdWords, Facebook, Instagram, LinkedIn, and display or remarketing advertising. Paid advertising is most effective when used to target people who are in the consideration or purchase phases of the customer journey.

Using the example from earlier of a side hustle that needs to generate $1,000 in the first month to be successful, a paid strategy may work quickly to acquire prospects who are more likely to turn into sales than the user who found your blog article on a specific topic useful from their Google search. Paid ads can work, but they come at a cost. As the term "paid" clearly implies, you are paying, typically per click or other action, for this traffic.

Engaging with potential buyers who are further along in the customer journey without having to nurture them over time can be a very good thing. But I don't recommend that most first-time side hustlers invest much money in paid campaigns until they've created a sales funnel and email marketing strategy, verified that their funnel works in converting leads into buyers, and can successfully track the results you're generating. Then and only then does it make sense to use paid ads to drive people into the top of your funnel.

A word of warning: there are a lot of misconceptions out there about Facebook Ads in particular. You may have seen the "expert" with the webinar promising how he or she can show you how to turn a $500 ad spend into six figures of sales from "cold traffic" (a term used to describe people who haven't heard of your brand or product before seeing your ad). Some of these "experts" will say that just by running paid Facebook ads you're all but guaranteed to become the next side hustle success story. What these folks don't always tell you is that the effectiveness of paid ad campaigns almost always comes down to having a proven, predictable, scalable sales funnel in place first. This is a topic for another book or course because there's just so much to cover. For our purposes, I simply want you to be astutely aware of the paid-ad pipe dream that's being sold online. I implore you to be patient and tread lightly if you do decide to try paid ads. Start small, track your results, and iterate.

There are tremendous resources out there that dedicate themselves solely to the art of paid digital marketing. I've listed some of my favorites below:

- Hubspot Blog
- DigitalMarketer.com
- Moz.com
- SearchEngineLand.com

Note: some resources offer organic tips as well.

Social Media

I have a love/hate relationship with social media. It can be both the greatest time suck on earth and the best return on investment you could ever dream of. Often, it's both at different stages. With social media, you can choose to rely on organic traffic, where you're simply posting and trying to build a following over time, or you can engage paid traffic on social media sites. On Facebook, for example, you have the option to "boost" a post that you posted for free to reach specific people.

Instagram and Snapchat have similar capabilities, as does Twitter (and basically every other social network).

The most successful social media marketers have created a proven strategy and exercised tremendous frequency and consistency over time. Social media marketing can be overwhelming because there are simply so many options. Just considering the multiple platforms and the types of content that are successful on each, building a strategy, creating the content, sharing it, and then actually engaging with your followers on a single platform can be overwhelming, let alone attempting to master multiple platforms. I recommend that first-time side hustlers choose one social platform and spend all their effort on that one platform to figure out what works before moving onto multiple audiences.

Depending on who you talk to, different brands, entrepreneurs, and side hustlers will tell you one platform is better than another, based on their experience. The reality is, you simply won't know what works for you and your business until you try. When you are deciding between platforms, think primarily about two things:

a) on which platform does my buyer persona already spend the most time, and b) is my competition also invested on this platform? Your initial reaction may be to go where your competition is not. After all, you may not be at their level yet, so why would anyone buy from you instead of them? However, I recommend you follow the leader and trust that their much larger teams and budgets have analyzed enough performance data to validate spending time and money on the platform in question.

Once you've created a social following and found ways to turn those followers into prospects and buyers, then and only then is it time to expand your social network presence.

Pro Tip: there are many tools that will allow you to have multiple social media presences and essentially cross-post or duplicate single postings to multiple platforms. If you insist on having multiple social platforms, or if you've already seen proven success and are ready to scale your social efforts, I would highly recommend you use one of these services to minimize the time investment in posting to multiple places. Buffer and Hootsuite are two of the industry leaders with relatively low costs that can help you achieve this.

Bonus Tip: although I don't recommend trying to leverage multiple social media platforms at the beginning, I encourage you to create accounts on all platforms to secure a consistent "handle" or username. When and if you do begin to use multiple networks, a consistent user name is key.

Email Marketing

Across all my various businesses and projects over the years, if there's one thing I wish I could go back and do differently, it would be this: invest great effort and focus into building an email list sooner.

As the forthcoming affiliate section will illustrate, there is simply no more valuable asset for a side hustler or entrepreneur than an accurate, clean, up-to-date email list of people who have opted in to receive your information. Donald Miller, CEO of Storybrand, estimates an email address provided by one of your prospects to be worth between $10-$15.[19] Whether you have a promotion coming up, a new product launch, or you're simply providing resources that your list will find valuable, the ability to land in your customer's inbox is exceedingly valuable.

In order to monetize your email list, you must have a strategy, and most strategies involve funnels. I could totally geek out on funnels and digital marketing here, but in the interest of time and value, I've provided a list of helpful email marketing resources in your workbook so you can focus on building your list and creating value for your personas.

Affiliates

If organic strategies take a long time to pay off, paid ads can be expensive and ineffective, and social media is a combination of the two, how does the first-time side hustler get their products or services in front of their buyer persona quickly, affordably, and profitably?

Affiliate marketing is one of the least understood but most valuable practices in digital marketing today. When done correctly, with a clear strategy and in partnership with the right people, it can be of tremendous value and exponentially decrease the time it takes to go from where you are to the success you're seeking in your side hustle.

To put it plainly, an affiliate is simply a person or brand who has already earned the trust of their followers or email list, who is willing to recommend or link to your product or service in exchange for some value, typically a commission.

Building a brand and an audience can be expensive and take time. But the moment someone joins your list usually isn't the moment to pepper them with hard sales copy. Once you begin attracting your audience, it may take time to build trust and nurture those relationships before new followers feel confident spending money for your product or service. If you're looking for a way to shorten this cycle and get to revenue faster, you'll want to pay special attention to affiliate marketing strategies.

The best affiliates are influencers who already have rapport with a significant number of your ideal buyer personas. Creating a relationship with a quality affiliate means that you won't have to pay out of pocket for the exposure and your offer can be placed in the inbox of thousands of your ideal buyers.

A solid affiliate relationship will leverage the trust and rapport that your affiliate partner has built with their audience over time, while adding significant and real value to their audience by introducing them to a product or service likely to help them solve a problem. Now this isn't "free" by any means, and finding great affiliates isn't always easy. The cost for affiliates to promote your "offer," as it's called in the industry, is typically a split of revenue that's sold to their audience, or as a result of promotion they do on your behalf. In many cases, the split is 50 percent or more of the gross sales that come via the affiliate's list or referrals.

While 50 percent may sound like a lot of money to give up to an affiliate, remember that you may not have any of it without their help.

To illustrate this point, let's use an example.

Let's say your goal is to sell 500 online courses per month for roughly $200 each to create $100,000 in monthly recurring revenue. If your email list contains 10,000 people and we assume an industry average email open rate of 2–3 percent and sales conversion rates of 10 percent, we could forecast that you would sell about 25 courses, creating $5,000 per month in revenue using your list alone. Now, that's great, and most people would be thrilled to build and market a digital course that created $5k per month on a recurring basis. However, as it relates to the stated goal of $100,000 per month, it's not nearly a large enough list.

A faster way to reach your goal would be to work with quality affiliates. By finding other marketers and influencers, with lists the size of yours or larger, and sharing 50 percent of the revenue, if you hit the target goal of selling 500 courses per month, your affiliates would earn a significant amount of money each month by promoting a course they believe adds value to their users. This is a win-win.

For the affiliate, they can gain goodwill with their users

by sharing something relevant to them without having to create, build, or market it themselves, and they earn a hefty commission for their efforts—in the case of our example, a healthy $50,000 per month.

Of course, it's also great for you because you would earn $50,000 rather than $5,000 without investing in paid ads, spending years growing your list, or convincing people you're as reputable as the person they already know, like, and trust. By tapping into the influence that other people have with your ideal persona, you can shortcut your path to exceed your revenue targets.

Getting Quick Wins

At this point, you should have a very clear picture of your new side hustle. You have clarity on what it's going to yield, how much time and resources you're going to put into it, how you're going to do it, who you're going to sell to, who you're competing with, the best content strategy to start with, and an initial marketing and sales strategy.

Now that you've put in all this time and effort, it is important to keep the momentum going and make sure you get a few quick wins to earn initial revenue from your new business.

This step is as much mental as it is tactical or strategic, and it isn't really about the amount of revenue you bring in or hitting your goals out of the park in your first week or two. Making your first sales and seeing real revenue flow into your new business bank account for the first time is about self-realization and the validation that you have transformed from the person you were when you picked up this book. You're moving from working in a job where you felt unfulfilled and at risk, daydreaming about "someday," to a person who has created something that adds a brand-new stream of revenue to your life. You've taken the first two steps to becoming *Unboxed*. Take a second and enjoy the moment!

THE CUSTOMER JOURNEY

Need More Help?

If this section has been valuable but you feel like you'd benefit from more detailed help, I recommend you check out my course *From Idea to Open for Business in 60 Days* at **www.nickmurphy.io**. The course walks through all the topics we covered in this section in even greater detail and provides access to live group coaching calls, lists of my favorite business resources to scale your side hustle, and more. The course will be most valuable to you if you find yourself committed to pursuing a side hustle, but you're still feeling overwhelmed, confused, or slightly uncertain about where to go from here. (When you enroll, don't forget to enter the code *Unboxed* at checkout to save 20 percent.)

Not everyone will need the course to be successful, and this entire section of the book was written to help those with the ability and drive to go it alone and still crush their goals. Regardless, I hope you found tremendous value in this section.

If you're fully committed to building and launching your side hustle, I really want to hear about your success! When you make your first sale or have a breakthrough moment, please find me on social media and use the hashtag #unboxedbook to share your successes with me. I can't wait to see what you'll do next!

"Have the courage
to follow your heart and intuition.
They somehow know what you
truly want to become."
—Steve Jobs

STEP THREE

BECOME YOUR OWN BOSS

By completing Step One and Step Two, you've already taken back significant control over your life and career. Your employer no longer holds all the leverage; you are earning money outside of your day job and you've developed skills and confidence that you may not have had before you started this journey.

Now that you're making the corporate world work for you and have developed a side hustle, it's possible that you no longer feel so unfulfilled at work because you're working towards a specific outcome that wasn't as clearly defined before. You may have a new perspective or purpose in your corporate career, and it's likely that as your side hustle continues to evolve, you'll become better and more strategic, allowing you to grow it in ways you didn't consider at the beginning. It's also possible you've tasted what life can be like outside of the corporate world and you're ready to break away and tackle life as a full-time entrepreneur.

There is no one-size fits all plan, and that is why the Step Three is optional. Becoming *Unboxed* isn't necessarily about going out on your own and becoming an entrepreneur. After all, entrepreneurship is hard and certainly isn't for everyone. Becoming *Unboxed* simply means that you now have the choice to walk away from your job when and if you feel the calling to do so. You've taken back control and you know hold the leverage. Congratulations!

If you are ready to embark on becoming a full-time entrepreneur and being your own boss, this section will help you avoid some of the most common mistakes entrepreneurs make that cost them time, money, and oftentimes their entire business. If you're not quite ready to go down this path, I believe you will still find value in the stories and lessons I share in the pages ahead as they can also be applied to your side hustle.

I've learned a lot of hard and expensive lessons along my entrepreneurial journey, and in this section I grade my first startup against the most important aspects of running a successful business to help you learn from my mistakes so that you can achieve success faster than I did.

LEVERAGE

STEP THREE

EMPLOYER   YOU

You Are Ready to Become a Full-Time Entrepreneur If:

- You can't imagine having another boss as long as you live
- You have honed in on a proven business idea that can grow to provide true differentiated value in the market AND quickly support you and your family financially
- You are OK taking big risks in the name of potentially big rewards
- You have developed IP (intellectual property) that can be licensed, sold, or developed

A Word of Caution

If I had to do it over again with all the knowledge I have now, I am not sure I'd choose this same path. At least not initially. That said, almost everything I've learned about start-ups, marketing, sales, building teams, raising capital, and more, came directly from the roughly decade-long journey of growing companies myself and figuring it out along the way.

This is the riskiest path of the three by far, so tread lightly and review the other sections if you haven't already embarked on your entrepreneurial journey. I chose entrepreneurship early on in my career, and in this section I'll share with you the good, the bad, and the ugly truth about my experiences. My hope is that you'll leverage my tactical advice to help get you started and that you'll find some early encouragement that you absolutely *can* build your idea into a company that gets acquired or even goes public.

How to Become an Entrepreneur

According to the Small Business Administration, 50 percent of new businesses fail within the first five years.[20] If your business is going to avoid becoming a statistic, there are a few things that are imperative to do well.

Create Differentiation

We talked in Step Two about how to create differentiation by understanding and researching your buyer personas and competition, doing a SWOT analysis, and understanding your place in the market. While there is money to be made in a "me too" business, it's not going to be enough to scale and become something that can be successfully exited from in terms of a major acquisition or IPO.

When you think about your business idea, try hard to create a truly differentiated product or service. But if you can't, don't beat yourself up over it. The reality is there are some businesses that are easier to differentiate than others. For example, if you sell water filters to homeowners, every one of your competitors' products is also going to filter water. There just isn't much room for uniqueness in terms of what the product does.

But if you can't easily differentiate your product or service from the competition in terms of function or purpose, focus on the next two sections and work to ensure you end up with a differentiated message for a specific segment of your market.

Solve a Big Problem for a Specific Audience

Jeff Bezos started Amazon by solving a specific problem for a lot of people. That problem, you ask? Having to go to a bookstore to buy books. Amazon created differentiation from brick-and-mortar bookstores by selling books online and delivering to our homes. Later, as technology evolved, their business added Kindle downloads and e-books and the possibility of self-publishing.

But even today, with as big as Amazon is and as many things as you can purchase from their platform, thinking about the use case of books is still a great example of how they began by solving a big problem for a specific audience by giving the public worldwide access to more titles than even the largest bookstores could ever carry in their inventory.

When analyzing the problem your business will solve, it's important to be honest with yourself and understand whether you're solving a big enough problem for a specific enough audience. Most entrepreneurs I see, especially first-time entrepreneurs, make the mistake of not thinking hard enough about this specific question.

Find a Niche

Most successful companies started in a niche market. Amazon didn't sell everything they could possibly sell or ship online; they started with books. Under Armour started as a company that sold apparel to be worn under football pads. The very first Under Armour shirt I ever saw was in 1999 when I was at Arizona State, long before it was a household brand that competed with Nike and Adidas. Even Apple, the world's first trillion-dollar company, started by making only computers. There was no app store, no iPhone, no tablet. They started out by building a superior personal computer and the success they found in that market, coupled with a brilliant and intuitive founder, led to their long-term growth.

There are many ways to niche down. You can niche down in geography, product, or audience. When you're initially building your business, ask yourself, is there a way that you can niche down further? As they say in the marketing world, "the riches are in the niches."

Have a Plan

In order to grow your business into something successful, you're going to need a plan. Actually, you'll need two types of plans.

The first type of plan is *financial*. You need a specific financial target in mind, not only about what the business needs to do financially to cover your costs but also what you need to take home in profits after taxes and expenses to support your lifestyle if you're going full-time as an entrepreneur out of the gate.

While I'm a big proponent of going out on your own even if it means taking a pay cut in the short-term, that pay cut can't be drastic, particularly if you have a family to feed. Your workbook contains a financial worksheet to help you quantify exactly how much money you'll need to make in your business to live the lifestyle that you're used to.

The second type of plan is a *strategic* plan. When you enter the market, who will you target as your first customers? At what price point are you going to position your product or service? Will you bring in a strategic partner to help you grow faster? There are all kinds of business strategy books that can help you articulate, plan for, and execute the best business strategy to fit the needs of your business. I've listed a few of my favorites here:

- *Blue Ocean Strategy* by Renee Mauborgne and W. Chan Kim
- *The One Thing* by Gary Keller
- *Good to Great* by Jim Collins
- *Leap: How to Thrive in a World Where Everything Can Be Copied* by Howard Yu

Be Honest with Yourself about Your Skill Set

Most entrepreneurs are really good at one thing, which is why they decide to start a business doing that thing. What they may not be good at is building technology, marketing, sales, customer service, finance, and any number of other things that an entrepreneur running a successful business must be able to understand, manage, and execute. Successful entrepreneurs are more than talented practitioners. They're skilled at leading people, communicating a clear vision, delegating, and managing.

I've included yet another exercise in your notebook to help you get clear on how to rank your own skill set in these critical areas. You'll notice as you look at the exercise that there's also a place for people that know you well to rank you. Therefore, this worksheet is designed to be a self-assessment, as well as an assessment by people who know you and have worked with you in the past.

Be sure to give the assessment to people you know will tell you the truth. For that reason, your mom or someone else who is going to say you're great at everything may not be the best person to survey. When you get the assessment back, look for trends rather than fixating on every answer. If you graded yourself a five out of five in a certain category, yet everyone else grades you a two, listen to them and work to understand the shortcomings they're perceiving. While they may be wrong about your abilities, they are not wrong about how you're perceived. Being honest with your skill set means you need to understand what you're good at, understand what you're not, own both, and don't be afraid to ask for help.

WorkBlast.com

The reason I'm so passionate about doing these five things well to build a successful company is because I didn't do any of those things particularly well in my first startup, and I want to help you avoid a similar fate.

I started WorkBlast.com with a co-founder back in 2006. It was a video resumé company designed to solve a problem I experienced when I was done playing football. We had identified a gap in the job search market and realized that adding a short video as a supplement to a text resumé gave people a better chance to tell their story. Our aim was to help people earn an invitation to the interview process where they could be in contention for a job offer.

My business partner and I were able to raise more than half a million dollars from friends and family. We created a tremendously successful media campaign with the help of a great publicist, in large part because the concept itself had everything that a PR company and news outlet would want: controversy, technology, seasonality, economics, and a futurist component to boot.

Getting media attention was never a problem for us. Our very first week in business, we actually co-sponsored *The Apprentice* season finale after-party at Le Deux Nightclub in Los Angeles, hosted by none other than Donald Trump. Articles about our concept were picked up everywhere from Yahoo to *USA Today* to the

Wall Street Journal and dozens of local and regional outlets across newspaper, radio, and TV.

Based on what you know so far, look into your crystal ball and tell me how you think it went from there. Most people presume that an idea to which people respond favorably is sure to be a financial hit and a very successful business.

I wish it were that simple. Considering the list of five things every business needs to do well to create a successful company, I've graded and reviewed my personal performance with WorkBlast.com.

Create Differentiation | Report Card: D

WorkBlast was conceptually differentiated, but the product never reflected that advantage. Back in 2006, broadband Internet was not available everywhere yet. There were no smartphones with built-in video cameras and cool video editing apps, and the idea of getting someone to sit in front of a video camera and understand what to say was nearly impossible to get to scale. In fact, when we would sit down to do our own video-resumé-type marketing for the site to educate the market, we would often be so uncomfortable that we would stop, take twenty or thirty cuts, and eventually put something out there that didn't look that great.

Solve a Big Problem for a Specific Audience | Report Card: C

If WorkBlast could have proven that our solution helped people to get more job interviews than traditional resumés alone, it absolutely would have solved a big problem. But for which audience? Were we targeting young professionals? Were we targeting sales people and marketers who needed to be seen and heard, so they could come across convincingly and compellingly? After all, their jobs depend on performing in front of people, something video could showcase better than text alone. Were we shortening the time to hire for recruiters themselves, providing more information and thus allowing them to vet a candidate more quickly?

We didn't realize it at the time, but having such a general value proposition was one of the biggest mistakes we made. The problem we were trying to solve was so big that we weren't able to gain the traction we needed to actually solve it for anyone.

Find a Niche | Report Card: F

As many first-time entrepreneurs feel, we thought our idea was the greatest thing since sliced bread. And everyone we shared it with tended to agree. "Oh, what a great idea," one person would say. "Who wouldn't use that?" someone else would say. "I'm going to tell my niece right now. She's looking for a job and she'd love it," added another person—but we never niched down. We never picked a geographic region, an industry, or even a specific segment of job seekers, like professionals early in their careers, for example.

If I had to do it over again, we would have done it very differently. We would have leveraged our location in the Phoenix market with graduates from Arizona State University, which just so happens to be one of the largest college campuses in the country by population.

We should have targeted young professionals like ourselves, people who could relate to our stories, whose path to getting noticed and interviewed is much more difficult than people with more business experience. We should have then niched down even further and focused on entry-level sales positions in the Phoenix market.

One of the most painful lessons I learned that drove this point home was a phone call I received after Work-Blast had generated national TV exposure. A talent acquisition director at a large department store chain called and asked, "How many retail store managers do you have in Baltimore?" While I don't remember exactly what I told the hiring manager, the answer was effectively zero. Had we understood the importance of niching down and proving our business with a specific segment, industry, or location, the outcome of the entire business may have been different.

Have a Plan | Report Card: C-

Our plan was to kick ass.

Our plan was to change people's lives.

Our plan was to make a lot of money.

That was the extent of our planning.

We had no specific budgets. While we were only paying ourselves $3,000 per month each, a conservative amount to be sure, we had absolutely no path to revenue to account for that salary burn, let alone the other costs we were incurring.

Our idea to wrap a 42-foot RV and use it to crash career fairs is, for my money at least, still the most epic guerrilla marketing strategy in the history of business. We made a splash. Job seekers and competitors alike took notice. Our bold marketing strategy generated hundreds of thousands of dollars in media exposure and brand awareness . . . but we didn't make a penny. We didn't know we needed to create and test an ideal buyer persona, and we didn't have a path to the consistent revenue we needed to prove market traction and raise the massive amount of additional money needed to become a national player in our space.

Be Honest about Your Skill Set | Report Card: B+

Looking back, this is the one area I feel we did understand who and what we were at WorkBlast. My co-founder and I were young and ambitious. We embodied the person who could benefit most from our solution and that made us passionate advocates for our business. While this may have helped us become great marketers, we were not great product engineers or software developers, and we certainly weren't great business executives, or people who should have been trusted with half a million dollars and no budgetary restrictions without more structure and oversight.

While we were conservative with the money, and by no means reckless, we did not have a plan and we didn't understand how much help we needed or how to go about asking for it from the right people.

Lessons Learned

I share all this with you not to relive the pain of my first startup failure, but to help you learn from my failures and missteps so you don't need to endure a similar fate on your way to entrepreneurial success. One of the things that helps me sleep well at night, even after having lost all of that money, is knowing what we knew then, we wouldn't have done anything different at the time.

As the saying goes, hindsight is 20/20, and one of my major hopes for this book is to help shape the way in which you look at your career, its risks, and its opportunities in the macro. I hope by reading this section you realize some of what not to do—because, let's face it, I made a lot of mistakes in that first startup. My business partner and I ran WorkBlast till the bitter end, where he lost his home and I filed for bankruptcy. That experience really did feel like a death in the family. While we both eventually became successful entrepreneurs, I don't want you to go through what we did if you can avoid it.

Lifestyle vs. Acquirable Entrepreneurship

There are dozens of types of companies you can build as a full-time entrepreneur. The majority of them fall into one of two buckets, defined by little more than your exit strategy: a *lifestyle business* or an *acquirable business*.

A *lifestyle business* is defined as a business set up and run by its founders, primarily with the aim of sustaining a particular level of income and no more, or to provide a foundation from which to enjoy a particular lifestyle.

An *acquirable business* is just that: a business that's set up from the beginning to be sold to another party or taken public (IPO).

While a smaller number of startups fall into the second bucket, this part of Step Three is dedicated to describing and educating you on the different things you'll need to do to build an acquirable business, from ideation to exit, while working on your company in a full-time capacity. Therefore, if you want to build a business to sell to someone or take public, or if you want to create more than $10 million in annual revenue at some point, pay special attention to this section.

Before we go any further, it's important to acknowledge that there are plenty of successful lifestyle businesses run full-time by their founder(s). Pat Flynn, a highly successful course creator, podcaster, and affiliate marketer, earned between $102,000 and $321,000 per month in 2017 alone.[21] Businesses like Pat's typically carry less risk, as these types of organizations are likely to have fewer employees and other fixed expenses to shed if either the business or founder experience hardships during the life of the business.

If your entrepreneurial endeavor seems more like a lifestyle business and you are fairly certain you do not want to sell your company to someone, take it public, build big teams, raise institutional capital, or deal with the headaches of running a large business, I'll direct you back to Step Two for the tactical elements of getting your lifestyle business off the ground. Just know that your mindset, your timeline, and your ability to execute will be different than the side hustler who's balancing all those things along with a full-time day job.

Proof of Concept

The tools required for success in a traditional start-up are very similar to what's required to create success in a lifestyle business. The key differences are the necessary amount of capital, speed of growth, and exit path.

If you want to build a large business as a full-time entrepreneur with the intent to sell it or take it public, you're going to need to prove your concept and get a minimum viable product (MVP) into the market before you're likely to raise any capital.

Proof of concept can vary from talking to 100 potential buyers and convincing 95 of them to say yes, to having a product on Kickstarter that gets shipped to 500 early adopters who help fund your campaign, and a million variations in between. No matter what your business is, you will have to show that there is a viable market for your product or service, understand your buyer persona, and have a strategy to make that persona aware of your offering, then differentiate it in a crowded market.

Proof of concept in an MVP will be absolutely critical if you need to gain investment capital to grow your business. But even if you don't, gaining that proof of concept or putting together an MVP will teach you valuable lessons and validate or destroy your assumptions as you begin down the path to growing your business.

FFF: Friends, Family, and Fools

Once you have proof of concept and a minimum viable product put together, you're likely to need some type of funding. The path of least resistance for most first-time entrepreneurs is often referred to as the triple F: friends, family, and fools. As the name suggests, they're friends of yours who believe in what you're doing and have the ability to invest in some capacity, family members with capital who want to see you succeed, or simply fools—i.e. the rich guy at the end of the block who thinks you're the next Steve Jobs. Friends and family rounds are usually good places to start if your capital requirement is between $10,000 and $100,000.

It was through this FFF channel that WorkBlast raised $500,000. We raised the money in increments of $50,000 from multiple people in our circle, from acquaintances to close family. When we needed more money later on in the company's life cycle, that same group of investors was eager to provide the next $50,000.

There are pros and cons to raising money from these types of investors.

Pros: It's usually a quicker sales cycle to get them to yes. They believe in you, they know you, they understand you, and you have more opportunity to talk to them about your business than you have with strangers and formal investors.

Cons: If you lose their money, you live with it forever. While an investment will always be an investment, and investments come with inherent risks, you never want to take anyone's money—stranger, friend, family, or even a fool—if you believe you will lose it.

I can tell you from experience that if the time comes that their money is gone and you're not able to return it, it's painful, frustrating, and sometimes awkward.

Let's Talk Co-Founders

When it comes to building your business, one of the very first decisions you'll make is whether or not you want to bring on a co-founder. As I've mentioned, I had a co-founder for WorkBlast, but my subsequent businesses have not included a co-founder. In my experience, there are pros and cons to each arrangement.

The Advantages to Having a Co-Founder

One major advantage in having a co-founder is that you have someone else to take the journey with. It's often been said that being an entrepreneur is one of the loneliest jobs in the world, and I can attest in a lot of cases it seems to be true. If you're working in your business alone, you may own 100 percent of the upside, but you also assume all the risks, all the stress, and you may not have anyone else who fully understands what you're going through on a day-to-day basis.

When you decide to bring on a co-founder, the relationship you build with them and with your early team members are frequently lifelong relationships. During the course of your business you will share the highest highs and the lowest lows and likely become very, very close.

In an ideal scenario, having a co-founder ultimately helps you fill a skill gap you don't possess yourself. A lot of teams are comprised of a technical founder and a non-technical founder. Depending on your type of business, one founder may bring the ability to write code, help build software, or design and run the machines required for your business, while the other co-founder understands marketing, sales, strategy, or other critical soft skills.

If you're committed to finding a co-founder, finding the person who is at the right season in their life, the right state of mind, and who is someone you would enjoy working with are all critical factors to consider.

However, the most significant factor in selecting a co-founder is choosing someone who not only checks all of the other boxes but who also has a skill set that is invaluable to your idea and long-term business growth.

Another advantage of having a co-founder is the access you gain to the other person's network. When the business needs funding, sales, contacts, or a board of advisors, you'll have another set of friends, family, fools, and relationships to choose from to help meet your company's goals.

The Downside of Working with a Co-Founder

Of course, having a co-founder in your start-up is not all sunshine and rainbows. Here are a few potential hurdles to be aware of.

The most obvious downside to having a co-founder is that you'll be splitting equity with someone else, even if the idea was all yours at the beginning. Typically, most partnerships maintain fairly equal equity parity. Founder splits like a 51/49 or 60/40 are common. And while the split shouldn't be 50/50, because someone needs to have the power to cast the deciding vote when you disagree, if you sell your business for $100 million, your take is going to be roughly half of what it would've been without a co-founder.

It's also worth noting that many partnerships fail. If you haven't seen the movie *The Social Network* about Mark Zuckerberg and the Facebook founding team, go check it out. Silicon Valley and businesses from around the world are full of stories about founding teams that didn't work out.

When you go into business with someone and it doesn't work out, the cost isn't simply a burnt relationship or the loss of a friend. Oftentimes these situations end with lawsuits that can cost you a lot of time, energy, and money that you should be pouring into your business.

Other Considerations

Treat your search for a co-founder as if it's a search for a spouse or a lifelong partner—because, in some cases, it may be. My relationship with my co-founder was such that four years after WorkBlast went under he was a groomsman in my wedding. While it takes a long time to build that type of relationship, it's imperative you know how the other person is going to behave in certain situations and identify any risks associated with relying on them as a partner long before you get into business together.

You'll also want to make sure your skills complement each other in your business. I just shared the example of the technical and non-technical founders, but if you're in a business that doesn't require technology, you'll still want each co-founder to bring their unique superpower to the business if it's going to grow. If you can do everything your co-founder can do, and they can do everything you can, then you probably don't need a co-founder.

At WorkBlast my co-founder and I had very similar skill sets. In fact, most of them overlapped. We enjoyed a lot of the advantages I mentioned above, in that we were able to expand our networks which led us to more investors and got us much further down the road than either of us could have gone alone. However, in the end we spent much of the money we raised hiring for the technical skill set we should have considered bringing on as a third equity partner from the beginning.

Growing a Team

Whether you decide to go it alone, bring on a co-founder, or seek out multiple co-founders to begin your business, at some point you're going to need to add to your head count in order to get things done and grow the company. There are two primary ways to get this done: hire employees or hire freelancers. Just like with the co-founder decision, there are advantages and disadvantages to both.

The Advantages of Hiring Employees

Perhaps the greatest single benefit to having employees is that they're 100 percent dedicated to a specific job inside your organization. If you build a good company culture, they're also likely to commit to your company and its stated mission.

Employees are typically more reliable than freelancers, and if you maintain a traditional office environment you're going to see the same people day in and day out. Over time you'll learn to trust each other and build a long-term relationship that can be nurtured and sustained.

When someone works for you full-time, even if they're not in the same office, you'll typically have smoother communication with that employee than you would with a freelancer. Eventually they'll understand your culture, learn your management style, and intuitively know what needs to be done. The best early employees quickly become autonomous and use their knowledge of the business and the founder's vision to solve problems and check off big goals without needing to be told exactly what to do.

If you're able to retain your early employees and develop them into leaders they can become passionate advocates inside your organization creating a huge cultural advantage if you scale your business to include dozens, hundreds, or even thousands of employees down the road. Many early employees become managers or executives inside their departments as the company grows, and those early employees help to reinforce your culture and your values and act as an extension of the founders themselves.

The Disadvantages to Hiring Employees

While having a dedicated full-time team of people working for you is great, there are some potential downsides to having employees.

Number one, they're damn expensive! Most companies with employees have office space. That means your business must account for the cost of rent, insurance, furniture, equipment, computers, internet, phones, mileage reimbursement matching taxes, benefits, retirement contributions, salaries, and the list goes on . . . and on . . . and on.

Additionally, very few new companies hiring their first employee or two are going to have any HR processes at all. They're not going to understand how to write job postings, they may not be skilled at interviewing candidates, and it's likely going to be an expensive, time-consuming learning process. There can also be costs associated with advertising your open jobs or finding a recruiter to help you attract and vet the right people to hire.

From a lifestyle standpoint, employees can also eat up a

lot of your day with the obligations of managing a team. It's imperative in young companies that the founder and co-founder are hyper-involved in everything as processes are being developed and the initial team is put in place and ramped up. This means early employees are going to need to be trained to learn the business, and in order to transfer knowledge you'll be pulled into frequent and important meetings with them each and every week, if not each and every day.

Because most founders and co-founders act also as full-time employees with a must-do list a mile long, spending too much time meeting with and training early employees can become a real drag on growth.

The Advantages of Hiring Freelancers

If growing your business doesn't necessitate having employees, or if you've simply decided you don't want to deal with having that kind of responsibility early on, take a hard look at freelancers. However, just like employees, just like a co-founder, and just like anything else in business, there are pros and cons.

A major benefit to hiring freelancers is the scalability

and availability of talented people who can do just about anything. You need a WordPress engineer? Done. A graphic designer? Done. A contingent recruiter? Done. An external sales team? Done.

You can add to, and then pull back on, the size of your teams to fit your business needs quickly and efficiently. Freelancers are also incredibly easy to budget for. Unlike employees, they're paid as 1099 contractors so there are no additional costs such as matching taxes, healthcare, retirement contributions, and so on. Because they're a 1099 contractor who sees higher net wages in the short term than W-2 employees do, occasionally you'll find some freelancers willing to work for less per pay period.

Tied directly to the scalability of freelancers is the ease of hiring and firing them. If you have a freelancer whose task is complete and you don't have more work in that area for a while, you simply let them go or stop their contract. Conversely, if there is too much work for one freelancer, you can easily add another.

But perhaps the most significant benefit to hiring free-lancers is gaining access to the best global talent for each specific task your business needs done. In my business today, I have an email marketing pro in Salt Lake City, a Search Engine Optimization (SEO) guru in Los Angeles, a developer in Beijing, a WordPress engineer in Islamabad, a brand manager in Minneapolis, a UX designer in Montenegro, a social media marketer in Florida, and four data scientists in Ukraine.

But before you get too excited, let's talk about the cons.

The Downside to Hiring Freelancers

Early on in your business, you'll likely be looking to freelancers to complete tasks that have yet to be done at your company. These are things like setting up your website, creating your collateral, building a social media following, etc. Freelancers are a great resource to help complete tasks you cannot do yourself. Learning to effectively vet freelancers, however, is an extremely important skill and can take time to master.

I struggled mightily with this in the beginning. When I needed someone to create a specific functionality in our technology, if a freelancer's application had quality client feedback and they told me they could get the job done, I really didn't have the skills to vet their capability or their understanding of the full scope of the project. Successfully vetting freelancers has become such a problem for startups that some companies do nothing but help small teams vet and hire contracted work.

To successfully hire freelancers, you must be able to scope your project and write great job postings. This can be challenging for several reasons. For example, it's unlikely that you have an HR background with the skills and experience to identify or create high-performing job postings with the knowledge of how to structure them or which message to focus on.

Unfortunately, it's impossible for any of us to know what we don't know. When I was hiring freelance developers for the first time, I understood the vision I was aiming for, but not the specifics around how best to build software to achieve it. Because I didn't know how to articulate proper benchmarks or properly scope the project in its entirety, it was virtually impossible for me to convey the full scope of the work in a job posting. More than once I found myself in a position where a freelancer was *convinced* they were finished with the project—and yet, it was only about a third of the way complete by my standards.

Perhaps the biggest downside to freelancers is most are simply not as committed as a partner or employee would be. Successful freelancers and contractors typically work on multiple projects at a time or have a list of clients waiting for them to free up and complete projects so they can move on to the next thing. This isn't always a bad thing, but it is something to be aware of when hiring freelancers.

Before You Hire, Consider . . .

Think through your business and ask yourself this question: "Do I need specialists or do I need generalists?"

It may be possible, for example, for a marketing manager to do a little bit of copywriting, a little bit of graphic design, and tackle basic social media marketing and SEO. For a single location business like my wife's dance studio, one person with that full skill set is probably more than adequate.

However, at WorkBlast we spoke directly to two types

of personas. On the B2B (business-to-business) side, we had to appeal to the needs of employers and people with jobs they needed advertised and filled. Yet, on the B2C (business-to-consumer) side, we needed to give value to the working professionals looking for their next great opportunity. Not only did the business have two audiences, but it was an online platform without a physical location so we needed to scale our message nationally—not an easy task.

Therefore, we needed specialists rather than generalists. We looked into hiring a content marketing guru as well as someone who could crush social media for job-seekers and someone who understood how to create compelling content pieces and get them in front of prospective employers and advertisers. The list goes on and on.

The Bottom Line

It's important to understand your needs. Can one person truly do everything you need them to do effectively with the budget you have, or would it be better for three or four specific experts to work remotely part-time to get the job done?

Pro Tip: when in doubt, start with a freelancer. In addition to being much cheaper and faster to get on-boarded—and easier to let go if it doesn't work out—having a freelancer will help you prove that the job you think is a full-time job is, in fact, a full-time job.

I can't tell you the number of times a project has felt urgent and I've thought, "Man, I really need a marketing executive to come in and do all of these things," only to realize during the course of the project that the business needs or my perspective had changed and it would be best to go in a different direction. If you go out and hire a VP of Marketing for $175,000 and things change quickly, like they often do in new businesses, your business can instantly find itself in a lot of trouble. When you test the waters with a proven freelancer, you can simply replace one freelancer's skill set with another if your needs change, or choose a different path entirely.

When you're first starting out, everything needs to be done for the first time, and it can seem overwhelming. Resist the urge to put someone in every seat at the onset. What I've found is that the needs of most young businesses pile up and drop off very quickly. The best advice I can give you at this stage is to keep your costs at a minimum and your flexibility at a maximum.

"Fear replaces the unknown
with the awful."

−Isaac Lidsky

CONCLUSION

O nce you've gotten your startup to this point, now the real work begins. From here on out, you're going to figure out how to grow your revenue, scale your business, and get to your exit strategy. Going deep in those three phases of business would necessitate an entire second or even third book. My goal with Step Three has been to give you what you need to answer your calling and get started on your entrepreneurial journey.

Most people never pursue a full-time startup even if they desire to be an entrepreneur. The path from startup concept to successful exit is complex and riddled with potholes, but if you have any hope of achieving your goal, you need to get started. Most entrepreneurs wait so long to get started that, in fact, many of them never do. They wait for the road to success to be fully mapped out as they sit in their garage, waiting for the magical day when there are no other cars on the road and every light along their path is green. Unsurprisingly, that day never comes and they never take the first step to creating their dreams.

This three-step plan is for doers. Doers don't try to create businesses in vacuums using fictitious crystal balls that never even remotely resemble the reality of working in their own startups.

I believe most people who work all the way through Step Three are either born entrepreneurs or became one early in life. The fact that you are considering the full-time entrepreneur path tells me a lot more about you than you may realize. Even if you haven't yet taken that first step to build your own business from scratch, inside you already have everything you need to succeed. You have the curiosity, drive, passion, ambition, risk tolerance, and maybe just that little bit of craziness that can make you a terrific entrepreneur.

Take it from someone who has started companies from

scratch, both failed and successful—I can tell you, as cliché as it sounds, all of the fun truly is in the journey. Reaching our goals is rewarding, but making progress towards our goals, learning, scratching the curiosity itch, and working with great people on a mission you're passionate about . . . That's what it's all about. If you've been waiting for someone to tell you that now is your time, or that you're ready, or that you deserve it, or that, yes, you can achieve your goals—quit waiting. You are ready to get started and be successful right now.

Steve Jobs wasn't Steve Jobs before he created Apple. In 1999, Jeff Bezos was just a guy in a solo office selling books online. And at one point Mark Zuckerberg was just another college dropout.

Companies are made; entrepreneurs are born. Now is your time.

Final Thoughts

Throughout the course of this book, we have covered a lot! We discussed many external factors unique to our time and place in the world and the impact that they could have on our lives, careers, and economies, and we've detailed the three-step plan you must take to *Unbox* yourself.

Hopefully along the way you've received some actionable tips to help you succeed in those endeavors. Regardless of the step you're working on right now, I want to encourage you to continue to do a few things to ensure your success and the success of others around you:

- First and foremost, continue to pay close attention to the world around you and defend against obvious risks to your job, career, or livelihood by playing great offense.
- Pursue aggressive risk mitigation strategies to help you build income and stability outside of your corporate job, remembering that your company wants you until the day they don't.
- Consider getting involved in local causes and seek to educate the next generation of workers. Help amplify the voices talking about the flaws and risks inherent within our current economic systems. New economic realities are emerging, and modern-day capitalism

may not be permanently sustainable in all western economies.

- Challenge your own limiting beliefs about what's possible for you in your career. Remember the power of recommitment and dedication and just how far those two simple principles can take you towards achieving your goals.

- Most importantly, I encourage you to know your worth, follow your curiosity, declare your intentions, and insist on living life on your own terms.

Whatever you do,

whatever you aspire to do,

#NeverSettle!

Nick

NOTES

1. "William Arthur Ward Quotes." BrainyQuote. Accessed December 18, 2018. https://www.brainyquote.com/quotes/william_arthur_ward_110212.

2. Gallup, Inc. "Dismal Employee Engagement Is a Sign of Global Mismanagement." Gallup.com. December 20, 2017. Accessed January 02, 2019. https://www.gallup.com/workplace/231668/dismal-employee-engagement-sign-global-mismanagement.aspx.

3. "The Wealth of Nations." Wikipedia. December 24, 2018. Accessed August 15, 2018. https://en.wikipedia.org/wiki/The_Wealth_of_Nations.

4. Ibid.

5. "The Recession of 2007–2009." U.S. Bureau of Labor Statistics. November 01, 2018. Accessed January 02, 2019. https://www.bls.gov/spotlight/2012/recession/pdf/recession_bls_spotlight.pdf.

6. Federal Reserve Bank. "Economic Forecasts with the Yield Curve." Federal Reserve Bank of San Francisco. March 5, 2018. Accessed August 17, 2018. https://www.frbsf.org/economic-research/files/el2018-07.pdf.

7. Nasiripour, Shahien, and Nicky Forster. "3 Charts That Show Just How Dire The Student Debt Crisis Has Become." The Huffington Post. March 23, 2017. Accessed August 17, 2018. https://www.huffingtonpost.com/entry/3-charts-student-debt-crisis_us_56b0e9d0e4b0a1b96203d369.

8. Manyika, James, Susan Lund, Michael Chui, Jacques Bughin, Jonathan Woetzel, Parul Batra, Ryan Ko, and Saurabh Sanghvi. "Jobs Lost, Jobs Gained: Workforce Transitions in a Time of Automation | McKinsey Global Institute." McKinsey & Company. November 2017. Accessed August 21, 2018. https://www.mckinsey.com/mgi/overview/2017-in-review/automation-and-the-future-of-work/jobs-lost-jobs-gained-workforce-transitions-in-a-time-of-automation.

9. Ibid.

10. Ibid.

11. Casselman, Ben. "Are Wage Gains Picking Up? Stalling? Questionable Data Makes It Hard to Say." The New York Times. March 12, 2018. Accessed August 11, 2018. https://www.nytimes.com/2018/03/12/business/economy/wage-data.html.

12. Wong, Patrick. "Are Wages Keeping Up with Inflation?" Glassdoor. January 30, 2018. Accessed August 02, 2018. https://www.glassdoor.com/research/are-wages-keeping-up-with-inflation/.
ALSO SEE:
Watson, Patrick W. "Real Wage Growth Is Actually Falling." Forbes. September 25, 2018. Accessed October 02, 2018. https://www.forbes.com/sites/patrickwwatson/2018/09/25/real-wage-growth-is-actually-falling/#2870f5b97284.

13. Casselman, "Are Wage Gains Picking Up? Stalling? Questionable Data Makes It Hard to Say."

14. Shepherdson, Ian. "U.S. | 5 December 2018 "Tariff Man" Doesn't Understand Tariffs That's Unfortunate." Pantheon Macroeconomics. December 05, 2018. Accessed January 02, 2018. http://www.pantheonmacro.com/documents/us-documents/i/5-december-2018-tariff-man-doesnt-understand-tariffs-thats-unfortunate/.

15. Denning, Stephanie. "Why The General Motors Layoffs Were Strategic." Forbes. December 01, 2018. Accessed December 03, 2018. https://www.forbes.com/sites/stephaniedenning/2018/11/29/why-the-general-motors-layoffs-were-strategic/.

16. Times Staff, Seattle. "The Motley Fool: GM Announces Layoffs, but Stock Rises." The Seattle Times. December 14, 2018. Accessed January 02, 2019. https://www.seattletimes.com/business/the-motley-fool-gm-announces-layoffs-but-stock-rises/.

17. Brown, Randy. "We're Not Job Hopping Enough, That's A Problem For Fed Chair Powell." Forbes. September 20, 2018. Accessed January 02, 2019. https://www.forbes.com/sites/randybrown/2018/09/20/were-not-job-hopping-enough-thats-a-problem-for-fed-chair-powell/#629a7f5a1ffc.

18. Loudenback, Tanza. "From Harvesting Honey to Cleaning Animal Skulls - Here Are 7 of the Most Unique Side Hustles." Business Insider. January 24, 2018. Accessed October 04, 2018. https://www.businessinsider.com/side-hustle-stories-from-chris-guillebeau-side-hustle-school-2017-12.

19. For further details, see http://storybrand.com or check out Donald Miller's StoryBrand podcast.

20. "Small Business Administration." Small Business Administration. August 2018. Accessed August 27, 2018. https://www.sba.gov/sites/default/files/advocacy/Frequently-Asked-Questions-Small-Business-2018.pdf.

21. Flynn, Pat. "Income Reports Archive." The Smart Passive Income Blog. December 2018. Accessed January 02, 2018. https://www.smartpassiveincome.com/income-reports/.

Made in the USA
Columbia, SC
15 December 2019

84966560R00143